"In a world awash in toxic mascul[...] es two important things. First, it unm[...] its implicit prosperity-gospel assumptions about sex, virginity, and marriage. Second, it reminds men that male sexuality preaches the embodied gospel truth that 'every man is called to be a father to the world in his own way.' Both of these truths are vital to healthy male sexuality. I commend *Non-Toxic Masculinity* to all the jaded Christian men who have been burned by purity culture and who are looking for a new yet distinctly Christian way forward."

Gerald Hiestand, senior pastor of Calvary Memorial Church and cofounder of The Center for Pastor Theologians

"Finally, a book that treats men like they can actually be full followers of Jesus! Zachary Wagner doesn't berate men, blame men, or condescend to men. He just tells the truth. The church has told a story of manhood that is toxic and looks nothing like Jesus, and the fruit has been rotten—broken, shame-filled men. Ruined relationships. Shattered women. But it doesn't need to be this way. By rediscovering what Christic manhood looks like, we can aim for emotional wholeness and health, especially in our sexuality. I'm excited to see men and women embrace this message!"

Sheila Wray Gregoire, podcaster at *Bare Marriage* and author of *The Great Sex Rescue*

"Boldly vulnerable, Zachary Wagner gives voice to the brokenness of male sexuality within contemporary Christianity, and in so doing he points the way toward healing. Because he is dogmatic only about the goodness of the gospel, readers from a broad spectrum are invited to join him as he continues to process the complexity of these issues. As one who advocates for the value of women in the Christian story, I am thrilled to recommend this book as one that restores and cultivates the God-given value of men."

Amy Peeler, associate professor of New Testament at Wheaton College and associate rector at St. Mark's Episcopal Church

"For millions of men shaped by evangelical purity culture, *Non-Toxic Masculinity* will be a breath of fresh air. Rather than offer lists of prohibitions and idealistic expectations, Zachary Wagner situates the conversation within a broader redemptive narrative—one that allows for imperfection while rejecting the dehumanization of women and men, one that decenters sexual morality without abandoning biblical guidance, and one that is filled with humility and grace."

Kristin Kobes Du Mez, author of *Jesus and John Wayne: How White Evangelicals Corrupted a Faith and Fractured a Nation*

"Zachary Wagner has written a book with perceptive insights about pop-evangelical cultures of sex and sexuality. Wagner writes from the cauldron of experience—his own and his wife's—to tackle topics of church abuse, ideologies of purity, and unwholesome habits of porn and promiscuity. Wagner gets to the heart of the evangelical 'sex problem' and offers an alternative vision of masculinity rooted in love rather than lust management. This is truly a Christian vision of masculinity that is desperately needed in a #MeToo and #ChurchToo era."

Michael F. Bird, academic dean and lecturer in New Testament at Ridley College in Melbourne, Australia

"I am so glad to see this topic being addressed with the necessary frankness, common sense, personal insights, and biblical wisdom that Zachary Wagner brings to these pages. I've no doubt that *Non-Toxic Masculinity* will generate fruitful and much-needed conversations that will serve the church and people for generations to come."

Karen Swallow Prior, research professor of English and Christianity and culture at Southeastern Baptist Theological Seminary, author of *On Reading Well: Finding the Good Life Through Great Books*

"Personal, vulnerable, well-researched, compassionately argued, and affirming of a grand biblical vision of manhood as the Lord intended, Zach Wagner's *Non-Toxic Masculinity* is a welcome gift to the church. Wagner de-weaponizes male embodied advantage and human sexuality so that we might have a vision of masculinity that honors the human dignity of all persons. Any man with a hopeful vision for exemplifying Christ as single or married, in any season of life, should consider Wagner's presentation of God-fearing, fully male manliness. Any believer who hopes to promote healthy, Spirit-empowered manhood to the generations to come should soak up the portrayal of God's redemptive vision for manhood in the pages of this work."

Eric C. Redmond, professor of Bible at Moody Bible Institute

"Sexual assault is one of the biggest issues facing the church. There are cultures that facilitate assault, and men bear responsibility for constructing and sustaining such cultures. For healing to occur, men must therefore repent from the toxicity of masculinity, and Zachary Wagner helps us take the first steps. Abusive power is healed by humility, chiefly demonstrated by Christ. Wagner's book both depicts and sets an example of this humility."

Fellipe do Vale, assistant professor of systematic theology at Trinity Evangelical Divinity School

ZACHARY WAGNER

NON-TOXIC
MASCULINITY

RECOVERING HEALTHY
MALE SEXUALITY

An imprint of InterVarsity Press
Downers Grove, Illinois

InterVarsity Press
P.O. Box 1400 | Downers Grove, IL 60515-1426
ivpress.com | email@ivpress.com

InterVarsity Press® is the publishing division of InterVarsity Christian Fellowship/USA®.
For more information, visit intervarsity.org.

All Scripture quotations, unless otherwise indicated, are taken from The Holy Bible, New International Version®, NIV®. Copyright © 1973, 1978, 1984, 2011 by Biblica, Inc.™ Used by permission of Zondervan. All rights reserved worldwide. www.zondervan.com. The "NIV" and "New International Version" are trademarks registered in the United States Patent and Trademark Office by Biblica, Inc.™

While any stories in this book are true, some names and identifying information may have been changed to protect the privacy of individuals.

The publisher cannot verify the accuracy or functionality of website URLs used in this book beyond the date of publication.

Cover design and image composite: David Fassett
Interior design: Daniel van Loon

ISBN 978-1-5140-0502-6 (print) | ISBN 978-1-5140-0503-3 (digital)

Printed in the United States of America ∞

Library of Congress Cataloging-in-Publication Data
A catalog record for this book is available from the Library of Congress.

29   28   27   26   25   24   23 | 12   11   10   9   8   7   6   5   4   3   2   1

To all the women who spoke up first

CONTENTS

PART III: GROWING UP, BECOMING A MAN

PREFACE

SHELBY WAGNER

ZACHARY AND I GOT MARRIED IN 2014. We had met five years before and, like most couples, felt there was nothing but joy ahead of us. We did not anticipate the issues of sexual intimacy that would plague our marriage. There were several reasons for these struggles, but a key factor was repressed sexual trauma. The body keeps the score even if the mind doesn't fully remember. This was certainly true for me, and we did not uncover the extent of my trauma until six years into our marriage. While I am quite open about my story of abuse, I won't go into the details here.

Since this revelation, Zachary and I—both as individuals and as a couple—have been on a journey toward wholeness and healing. Through this process, we have developed a shared concern and passion for Christian communities: the church must foster an atmosphere of authenticity and openness surrounding things we have always been told (implicitly or explicitly) to keep hushed, namely, the "darker" sides of our humanity. I am so proud of my husband for his vulnerability in this way.

Zach and I are sensitive to the too-prevalent pattern in the church of men speaking for women. We thus feel it is important that you readers hear directly from me, as there is much in this book that concerns my own experiences. So, know from the outset that I give my enthusiastic support and consent for the inclusion of every part of my story you'll read in these pages.

I believe this book has a beautiful and powerful message. My hope is that as you read it, you find encouragement and healing regardless of where you are in your own journey.

INTRODUCTION
WAKE UP, GUYS

IT'S A CONFUSING TIME TO BE A MAN.

The #MeToo movement began in 2017 with sexual abuse allegations against Hollywood producer Harvey Weinstein. More and more women began sharing their own stories of abuse, first in Hollywood and then in all sectors of society. This deluge of courage and solidarity brought the issue of sexual violence against women to the forefront of our social consciousness. A cultural debate ensued, as prominent and well-beloved men fell to accusations one after another.

These conversations reached a fever pitch the following year when Dr. Christine Blasey Ford came forward and testified before Congress that US Supreme Court nominee Brett Kavanaugh had sexually assaulted her decades before. Millions of Americans, myself included, sat glued to their screens for both Dr. Ford's testimony and Justice Kavanaugh's impassioned self-defense. On that day, Kavanaugh was in the hot seat. But ever since, men and masculinity, broadly construed, have been under scrutiny and examination.

Another high-profile case involved Stanford University student athlete Brock Turner, who was convicted of sexual assault at nineteen years old. Turner served only three months in prison, but some felt the public outrage against him and his new status as a registered sex offender ruined his life prospects. In response, the young woman Turner assaulted, Chanel Miller, spoke powerfully during a victim impact statement, saying,

> I want to show people that one night of drinking can ruin two lives. You [Turner] and me. You are the cause, I am the effect. . . . He is a lifetime sex registrant. That doesn't expire. Just like what he did to me doesn't expire, doesn't just go away after a set number of years. It stays with me, it's part of my identity, it has changed the way I carry myself, the way I live the rest of my life.[1]

Responses to these and other scandals of sexual misconduct have been varied and often polarized. Many see a struggle for cultural progress, a noble battle in the ongoing fight for women's liberation. Some question the reliability or motives of the women coming forward with allegations of abuse. Some respond with genuine sadness, but partially dismiss the phenomenon, saying "boys will be boys"—suggesting male sexual violence is an inevitable part of society. Some respond with fear that they themselves or a man they love could become a "victim" of public outrage and hatred because of such an accusation.

These scandals are understood by some to be a consequence of toxic masculinity, which is a shorthand way of referring to the unsavory and dangerous aspects of our cultural concept of maleness. *Toxic masculinity* describes men and boys who are emotionally repressed, egotistical, macho, and immature. It produces and perpetuates a male sexuality characterized by erotic conquest, entitlement,[2] objectification of women, violence, and a lack of self-control. This concept of maleness, it is argued, primes men to become predators.

There's broad agreement that men should not be like this, which raises the question, What *should* men be like? What is "non-toxic" masculine sexuality? Many agree that consent is a good starting point, but no further consensus has emerged in the cultural conversation, leaving even sincere and well-intentioned men confused about their own identity and the appropriate expression of their sexuality.

THE CHURCH TOO?

The #MeToo movement hasn't been limited to the secular world. Since the sexual revolution of the 1960s and '70s, evangelical Christians have been at pains to differentiate their vision for human sexuality from permissive and liberated attitudes in the broader culture. The "Biblical Manhood and Womanhood" movement championed the nuclear family, marital fidelity, submission and motherhood for women, and leadership and hard work for men. Another wave of evangelical responses involved a slew of popular books on sex, dating, and marriage, the most influential of which was Joshua Harris's *I Kissed Dating Goodbye*, published in 1997. The movement that gave rise to these books is often referred to today as "purity culture," which is characterized by a rejection of typical dating and a strong emphasis on premarital abstinence and moral sexual purity.

The stated goals of these movements have been to uphold Christian values against secular ones and to protect God's people from the moral stain and consequences of sexual immorality. Christians have often presented themselves as having the moral high ground as it relates to sexuality, but has this proven to be true? Have biblical manhood, biblical womanhood, and an emphasis on sexual purity spared the church from the scourge of toxic masculinity? The answer to this question—tragically, but clearly—is no.

In late 2017, Emily Joy Allison, a survivor of church-based sexual abuse, helped launch #ChurchToo, a parallel hashtag to the viral #MeToo. This and the related #SilenceIsNotSpiritual hashtag brought to light hundreds of stories of abuse, assault, and cover-up in churches and Christian organizations. Months later, a *Houston Chronicle* exposé cataloged hundreds of instances of sexual abuse in Southern Baptist (SBC) churches.

Bill Hybels, senior pastor of Willow Creek Community Church, one of the largest and most influential churches in the world, resigned in 2018 amid allegations of sexual misconduct. Many other high-profile pastors have fallen to sexual scandal in recent years, including Billy Graham's grandson Tullian Tchividjian and Hillsong Pastors Carl Lentz, Darnell Barrett, and Brian Houston. Other pastors like CJ Mahaney, John MacArthur, and Mark Driscoll, while not themselves accused of sexual abuse or misconduct, have been at the center of controversies involving abuse, cover-ups, or toxic cultures of masculinity.

Several horrific stories broke in quick succession in early 2021. On February 11, *Christianity Today* published the findings of an investigation detailing numerous instances of sexual abuse and assault by world-renowned apologist and evangelist Ravi Zacharias. Days later, a twenty-one-year-old member of a Southern Baptist Church went on a killing spree at massage parlors in the Atlanta area. While being questioned by police following his arrest, the shooter cited his "sexual addiction" as his motive. He targeted the women at these massage parlors—the majority of whom were of East Asian descent, women routinely fetishized in American culture—to "eliminate his temptation" to sin. In April, Josh Duggar (the eldest son of the Duggar family of *19 Kids and Counting*) was arrested on child pornography possession charges.

The stories and scandals keep coming. In 2022, *Christianity Today* published an exposé of sexual harassment in its own offices. Later that year, an independent investigation of the SBC revealed the pattern of sexual abuse and cover-up was far more pervasive even than the *Houston Chronicle* had shown. And, sadly, the scandals mentioned here are just scratching the surface.

Christians have responded to these and similar stories with deep embarrassment and alarm. In one sense, embarrassment is appropriate, but such shame is useless if it does not lead to repentance and change. Embarrassment alone can actually be harmful if it causes us to cover up or excuse our sin—like Adam hiding from God in the garden.

Many have noted with sadness that the sins of these men have compromised the witness of the church and destroyed ministries that had won many to Christ. But the church's evangelistic mission should never be at the expense of victims who are traumatized by suffering and abuse. If the preaching of good news comes with violence and dehumanization at the hands of the preachers, is it still "good" news? Jesus told his disciples, "Watch out for false prophets. They come to you in sheep's clothing, but inwardly they are ferocious wolves. By their fruit you will recognize them" (Mt 7:15-16). The ravenous wolves are not those who deny the gospel through false doctrine, but those who deny the gospel through their sinful conduct.

WHEN THE SUBCULTURE BEARS BAD FRUIT

But this isn't just about pastors. The fracturing of institutions often involves abuse and domestic violence perpetrated by church elders, lay leaders, and attendees. The knee-jerk response to these situations has often been to guard the leader. Keep it quiet. Protect the institution. Is this the appropriate response? Paul exhorts the church in Ephesians, "Have nothing to do with the fruitless deeds of darkness, but rather expose them" (Eph 5:11). Have we done everything we can to root out this wickedness? Any refusal to confront the epidemic of sexual sin and violence infecting our churches is an indictment on all of us, not just the perpetrators of the most heinous crimes. As Jackson Katz puts it, "Men are not only the primary perpetrators of gender violence. We are also the not-so-innocent bystanders."[3]

Our first response should be to grieve for and with the countless women, men, and children who have been harmed, abused, victimized, and raped by men who claim the name of Christ. The path of care and advocacy for these victims includes holding their abusers accountable by both church discipline and legal measures. We can no longer tolerate the routine victimization of women and children by men in our churches. It never should have been tolerated in the first place.

Is it any wonder that the broader culture has a hard time taking evangelicals seriously when we speak about sex, gender, and marriage? Our house—God's house—is not in order. It has become clear that the church is not in a moral position of strength from which to speak to the culture about human sexuality. They have known us by our fruits.

Some of you might be thinking, *Not all Christian men are abusers!* Yes, and thank God for that. I don't believe, as some do, that most Christian men are actively trying to maintain a system of power-hungry patriarchy. I don't believe Christian men are indifferent to sexual sin and the suffering of women. On the contrary, I believe most Christian men see sexual sin as serious in their own lives as well as in the lives of others. Most Christian men are genuinely, even deeply grieved by violence and abuse. Most Christian men do not want to succumb to temptation, much less become predators.

But why is it that so many Christian men fall short of their own ideals? Why is it that an insidious, toxic masculinity has found a safe haven in our churches, hidden behind a veneer of respect for women?

The church as an institution is sick. Some may object, "It's not the church that's sick, it's the culture!" But the church should be better than the culture in this regard. As Christians, our first and primary concern should be the righteousness of the church community. As the apostle Paul wrote in response to a sexual scandal in Corinth, "What business is it of mine to judge those outside the church? Are you not to judge those inside? God will judge those outside. 'Expel the wickedness from your own community'"[4] (1 Cor 5:12-13).

EVERY MAN'S BATTLE

The scandal of abuse in the church is every Christian man's problem. Even if we ourselves are not abusers, we are not precluded from having participated in the subculture that produces and shelters abusers with alarming regularity. Is simply not being a predator where the bar is set for Christian leaders and Christian men? Surely, we can do better than this. The victims of these crimes are image-bearers of God, our sisters and brothers in Christ and coheirs to the kingdom. If you are in Christ, this is your problem—and you should be part of the solution.

We now bear a sober responsibility of asking hard questions. What has gone wrong with Christian men? More specifically, what has gone wrong with the sexuality of Christian men? Even those of us who are innocent of abuse may not be as guiltless on these issues as we may think. As sinners, all men fall short in many ways. Would any man be so bold as to claim he has never sexually mistreated a woman? If you're a man, it's worth taking a moment and asking yourself how your wife or even your girlfriend (or former girl-friend) would answer the question of whether you've ever wronged or harmed her in any way sexually.

Sexual frustration and unhealthy, sinful modes of sexual be-havior remain all too prevalent. This isn't just about violence and abuse. Despite speaking out against pornography, Christian men still use pornography at alarming rates.[5] Many married Christian women report low levels of sexual satisfaction.[6] Divorce rates among evangelicals are higher than among other religious groups in America.[7] Christians who would like to be married remain con-fused about the "right" way to date.

The fight against sexual brokenness involves more than an individualistic fight against temptation. It is a fight for justice on behalf of the men, women, and children who have been dehumanized by a deficient and sub-Christian view of what it means to be a man. It is a fight against the contagion of toxic masculinity that has infected the church. Expelling this wickedness from our communities is, indeed, every man's battle.

WHO THIS BOOK IS FOR

This is a book about male sexuality and, particularly, what has gone wrong with male sexuality in conservative evangelical churches. Even more specifically, this is a book about how purity culture has—despite the best intentions of many—contributed to the cultivation of toxic masculinity in the church. I want to suggest that this broken masculinity is not merely a failure to live up to purity culture's ideals, but is, to some extent, the result of purity culture itself.

In these pages we will explore how the church has imported many of the wider culture's unhelpful ideas about sex and masculinity. We will also see how it mixes these assumptions with poor theology and sub-biblical ideas about humanity, redemption, sin, and temptation.

I have written this book primarily for men because it is men who need to change their attitudes and behaviors around sex. But I hope many women will read it too. I hope advocates for victims of abuse will read it. I hope mothers of young daughters and sons will read it. I hope it will be a helpful resource for pastors, leaders, and theologians.

The cultural criticisms of this book are not an exercise in man hating. They are instead a serious call for male accountability. Doing so is actually pro-male, because holding men accountable comes from an earnest desire to make men better. But beyond accountability, the church and our culture desperately need a positive vision for masculinity. Some argue that Piper and Grudem's "biblical manhood" is this vision. In recent years, I have come to have serious doubts. We must face the fruit of our current conception of masculinity and, where necessary, reevaluate our assumptions. If our Christian culture's masculine ideals tend toward frustration, sin, scandal, and abuse, maybe they aren't so biblical after all.

I also hope that some who have rejected the church, evangelicalism, or a historic Christian sexual ethic may find help in this book. If you're critical of the church, I want you to know that I am too. I am deeply disturbed by the behaviors and patterns of thinking about male sexuality in Christian circles. My love for the church remains, but I understand if you find it difficult, even impossible, to be part of the worshiping community. I have written this book because I care about the church. I have also written this book because I care about those who have been wounded and scarred by the church in this regard. I see you. And I am so sorry. I hope this book plays a small part in preventing others from experiencing the pain you have endured.

I recently asked a friend of mine why she no longer identifies as a Christian. She answered without hesitation: "Sexuality—LGBTQ rights, abuse, patriarchy. The whole thing. It's 100 percent because of sexuality." Many have had enough of the dysfunction they see infecting the church. Sexual hypocrisy, abuse, and cruelty are the reasons so much of my generation has left the Christian faith altogether. I confess that I feel that tension too.

Which brings me to the last person I have in mind writing this book—myself. This is a personal topic for me for multiple reasons, and I hope to be honest and open about my own struggles, questions, and difficulties in this area of my life. In recent years I have come to believe that the church itself instilled and confirmed in me many unhelpful and untrue ideas about God, myself, men, and women. The church did not always provide me with healthy attitudes toward my sexuality and sexual sin. Purity culture did not equip me for sexual suffering and difficulty in marriage. I was taught to avoid sexual temptation and sexual sin, but I was given few resources for understanding why I found sexual sin enticing. This focus on outward righteousness and behavior modification left me woefully unprepared to love my wife well as she wrestled with the difficult revelation of deep wounds from childhood sexual abuse. Throughout this book, I'll share various pieces of our story, and I want you to know from the outset that everything I share is with Shelby's full support and consent.

WHO MADE THIS BOOK POSSIBLE

Several books have been published critiquing purity culture in recent years. Thus far, these have been almost exclusively written by women, which is perhaps not surprising, as women have suffered the worst fallout from the Purity Movement.[8] It's high time for men to follow in their steps and join the conversation. We men need to own our responsibility in the pain that's been caused and how we have passively (or actively) participated in it. These pioneering and courageous women have led us well in writing prophetically against injustice and calling our attention to this dysfunction. I am greatly indebted to them and their trailblazing example.

Before reading and hearing from these women, I didn't understand how the mainstream evangelical vision of masculinity was hurting people. I didn't realize certain attitudes toward sexual sin place all the responsibility on women rather than men. I didn't realize that what I thought were biblical ideas were repackaged cultural misogyny and that I was reading the Bible and church history wrong. So much of what I've learned about sexual brokenness in the church I've learned from women who were courageous enough to say to the men in their lives, "You're hurting us." This book is a work of gratitude to these women—and an apology. Ultimately, this book exists because my wife, Shelby, told me that I was causing her pain—that my sexual neediness, immaturity, and entitlement was harming, even retraumatizing her.

I've learned so much on these issues from so many women. One of today's loudest and most effective critics of broken masculinity is Rachael Denhollander, who was instrumental in bringing US Olympic Team doctor Larry Nassar to justice for abusing her and scores of other young athletes.[9] She remains a resilient and effective advocate for survivors as a lawyer, writer, and public speaker. She is also a committed Christian and speaks regularly against sexual abuse in the church. On May 7, 2021, she wrote the following in a post on Facebook:

> We don't think [sexual violence is] a big deal in Christian culture because we've also peddled the "boys will be boys" mindset. Except we've added Scripture to it, and told women they're responsible for men's lust and addictions. That if they don't have sex enough, his needs won't be met and he'll stray. We've talked about his sexual needs like it's impossible to go more than a few days without release, but couched her sexuality as existing solely for his benefit. We've turned women into dangerous beings who control whether men "fall," and also into the solution for it. And yes, defining women and sexuality this way is the norm, it's not the exception. Telling women to be more sexually available to help their husband keep it in his pants is the norm, not the exception. Women are taught as the cause and solution to men's sexual perversions.
>
> Until our theology changes to actually reflect Scripture, we shouldn't be surprised at any of this. It's a story I see every single day. It's wicked. It's evil. And it's long past time that we called it that—not just the abuse, but the twisted theology that fuels it.[10]

We need to do more than bring abusers to justice. This rot goes deep. The broken masculinity we see in the church isn't just about a few bugs in the system. It's baked into our theology. And dehumanizing theology leads to dehumanizing behavior. We need to

PART I

PURITY CULTURE AND THE ROOTS OF TOXIC MASCULINITY

ONE

WHAT IS "PURITY CULTURE"?

A BRIEF GENERATIONAL HISTORY

I FIRST READ *I KISSED DATING GOODBYE* when I was eleven. I remember the cover clearly. It depicts a well-dressed man wearing a fedora, head tilted forward, face obscured beneath the shadow and rim of the hat. I also remember the back cover, which shows the author, Joshua Harris, face no longer obscured, looking up toward the camera from a relaxed, crouched position on the ground. To my pubescent, homeschooled brain, there was something admirable and cool about Harris. His handsome features and demeanor were striking to me. I saw a man who had journeyed through the turbulent teenage years of sexual and relational development and emerged unscathed and respected by his family, peers, and the broader Christian community.

Boy Meets Girl, the sequel to *I Kissed Dating Goodbye*, tells the story of Harris's courtship with his future wife, Shannon. This cover consists of two romantic and wholesome photographs of the young couple, one on the front and one on the back—apparent paragons of Christian sexual virtue, blessed by God with joy, peace, and security in their relationship.

I internalized the anti-dating rhetoric of these and other books, and I aspired to the joyful future that Harris and others held out in front of me. As a tween, I remember having what seemed at the time to be high-stakes discussions with friends about whether "going out" was a sin. My parents and I shared an understanding that dating was dangerous and to be avoided, especially with non-believers. I also remember wondering about the earliest age at which I could expect to get married, since being ready for marriage was, after all, the only context in which you could allow yourself to explore a connection with someone of the opposite sex. Thoughts like these regularly swirled in my twelve-year-old brain.

There were other books: *Passion and Purity, When God Writes Your Love Story, Sex Is Not the Problem (Lust Is), For Men Only, Real Marriage.* The list goes on, and I read them all, but certain books loomed larger than the others. Purity culture is often most associated with Harris's anti-dating rhetoric, but Arterburn and Stoeker's *Every Man's Battle* was, I believe, even more influential in the formation of Christian young men during the Purity Movement and beyond. In my conversations with various men in preparation for writing this book, *Every Man's Battle* came up over and over. I could spend a lot of time quoting from and critiquing the views of sexuality in *Every Man's Battle*, but others have already done an excellent job dismantling purity culture classics.[1]

Purity culture wasn't just about the books. It was and is a *culture*. Often people were more shaped by face-to-face relationships with parents, pastors, and peers who spoke to them in even more unhelpful ways than the books. A youth pastor doesn't have his sermon filtered by an editing process or a publisher. Parents aren't held to the standard of public discourse when they reprimand their children about dating. Your fifteen-year-old friend had no idea what he was talking about when he told you making out with your girlfriend would ruin your future marriage. The logic of purity came fast and thick for many growing up in the church during those years. What are some of the historical factors that gave rise to this culture?

DEFINING PURITY CULTURE

Purity culture was most prominently expressed in the Purity Movement of the 1990s and 2000s, a movement centered in America and spearheaded by evangelical, white, politically and socially conservative Christians. Books and conferences played a significant role, but the strong emphasis on sexual purity was never limited to them. It existed before, and it continues to exist afterward.

Purity culture involves more than a specific view of sexual ethics. For instance, the view that sex should be reserved for marriage has been around for as long as human civilization. This is not a uniquely Christian perspective. Extramarital abstinence has been (and continues to be) advocated for by people of many faiths, including Judaism and Islam, as well as those subscribing to no faith at all. Yes, people have always had sex outside of marriage, but the moral norm of abstinence is much larger than a Christian movement of the past few decades.[2]

Rather, purity culture is a cultural movement that defines itself in opposition to a wider cultural movement, the sexual revolution. Purity culture is not only characterized by the *what* of evangelical sexual ethics. It is also about the *why* and the *how*.

Here's how I define the term: *Purity culture refers to the theological assumptions, discipleship materials, events, and rhetorical strategies used to promote traditional Christian sexual ethics in response to the sexual revolution.* We'll get into more of the details of purity culture teaching in chapter two. For now, we can summarize by saying it was characterized by a strong emphasis on (1) premarital sexual abstinence for young people, (2) sexual freedom and fulfillment within heterosexual marriage, and (3) the assurance of blessing for those who lived according to this ethic and consequences for those who transgressed it. Again, purity culture is not co-extensive with the Purity Movement. It involves many other interconnected strands of the recent evangelical story, ranging from the Council on Biblical Manhood and

Womanhood, to Quiverfull, to Focus on the Family, and to Mars Hill Church in Seattle.

Rooting out toxic masculine sexuality in the church isn't simply a matter of correcting some of the excesses of teen-targeted rhetoric from the 1990s. This story is much bigger than that.

A GENERATIONAL HISTORY

The messaging of the Purity Movement didn't come out of nowhere, and understanding the past is an important part of understanding the present. As we look around at the ongoing sexual brokenness in individual Christians, pastors, and churches, we would do well to ask ourselves hard questions about our history as American Christians. Only then can we begin to explore how we might change course and become a different type of church with a different type of men. I offer here a brief generational overview of the Purity Movement in American Evangelicalism.

Baby boomers—Authors of the sexual revolution. The years following the end of WWII were characterized by optimism, economic growth, and babies.[3] Many Americans still romanticize the 1950s. With no more enemies to fight, men returned home to an American paradise to enjoy their well-earned freedom and peace. At the center of this idyllic American life was the family: a happy and adoring housewife tending to beautiful, well-mannered, well-dressed children. This is the era of *Leave It to Beaver*. A respectable and hard-working man could expect to come home from work every evening to marital bliss.

However, the world baby boomers were born into is not the world they came of age in. While the causes and effects of the sexual revolution of the 1960s and '70s are complex, a rejection of traditional marriage and family morality was at its heart. The existential threat of nuclear war, a new wave of feminist ideology, and the introduction of the birth control pill combined to release a world-shaking force of youth liberation. The familial, sexual paradise built around a central father figure grew unappealing to the emerging generation. Historian Doug Owram writes, "Of the many ironies in the history of the baby boom, the most prominent is that it, a generation [baby boomers] which so often scorned the ideals of family and home, was descended from a generation that valued home so much."[4]

The sexual revolution turned the world upside down.[5] There has never been anything quite like it in world history. Its effects are felt today and will continue to be long into the future. For example, during this period, many women came to see traditional sexual systems as oppressive and repressive. They took ownership of their sexuality and reproduction in unprecedented ways. LGBTQ+ people began to coalesce into a community for the first time. New forms of contraception made casual sex more common and, supposedly, less risky. Baby boomers charted a new course for sexual attitudes and behavior.

In other ways, though, boomers weren't that different from previous generations. By the 1980s, the Vietnam War had ended, and the threat of nuclear war and communism was beginning to wane. Baby boomers were now established adults, and many got married and had children and bought houses with yards in the suburbs. Some began to speak out against the sexual permissiveness of the new Western culture. Christian leaders warned that American society would soon collapse due to moral decadence, the same thing, they argued, that had caused the fall of the ancient Roman Empire. These leaders saw the fallout of the sexual revolution wreaking havoc in society—out-of-wedlock births, teen pregnancy, divorce, fatherlessness, STDs, and AIDS. Many felt they needed to fight back against these cultural forces, providing an alternative to sexual liberation. A renewed emphasis on "sexual purity" emerged.

This movement was not, in my view, a simple return to biblical or historically Christian principles about sex. It was primarily a reaction against the sexual revolution. Historic Christian assumptions about sexuality were being challenged and rejected at a rate never seen before. To combat this trend, a slew of Christian organizations appeared with particular emphasis on "family values."[6] On the surface, the emerging emphasis on sexual purity was a well-intentioned attempt to mitigate people's suffering by commending God's design for human sexuality. However, I will argue that many of the theological and cultural foundations of the movement were sub-Christian, even worldly.

Generation X—Promoters of sexual purity. In the second half of the twentieth century, sex and family were seen as central battlegrounds for the soul of America.[7] In this sense, the story of the Purity Movement was spurred on by Christian Nationalism,[8] a belief that the United States is a Christian nation, chosen and blessed by God, and that it is the responsibility of the church and individual Christians to make sure it stays that way.

But the Purity Movement wasn't just about protecting the soul of America. It was also about protecting the souls of individual children and young adults. Christian parents whose children were born in the 1980s and '90s wanted something different, better, for their kids. Generation X (born 1965–1980) was deployed by the Christian subculture to promote the ideas around sexual purity as a response to the sexual revolution. Historian Sara Moslener writes,

> Just twenty years prior, young people of a different generation were known for publicly declaring their right to sexual freedom. The new 1990s youth evangelicals, schooled in the destructive consequences of sexual excess, likewise found themselves fueled with political and spiritual fervor and able to find a national stage.[9]

These emerging adults served as mediators between baby boomers and their children, the millennials.

Christian musical artist Rebecca St. James was a notable Gen X proponent of purity values. Her song "Wait for Me" captured the hearts and imagination of young Christian girls who envisioned a handsome, noble young man "waiting" to marry them. Singing from the male perspective, the rock-rap hybrid group DC Talk included two purity-themed songs ("I Don't Want It" and "Kinda Girl") on their 1992 album *Free at Last*. But, the most prominent of these Gen X proponents of purity culture was Joshua Harris himself, whose books became emblematic of the movement. *I Kissed Dating Goodbye* sold over one million copies.

Millennials—The children of purity culture. Though the seeds of purity culture had been sown and were bearing fruit as early as the 1980s, it was in the 1990s and 2000s that the movement reached its height. Thus, millennials, the generation born between 1980 and 1995 are at the center of purity culture's consciousness. I was born in 1991 into a generation of white evangelical Christianity with a fully developed and carefully maintained machine of pro-abstinence rhetoric and resources.

My youth group experiences included several multi-week teaching series about sex, dating, and saving yourself for marriage. Every two years, my church would host hundreds of students for a "Purity Retreat" at a camp in Michigan—three full days on nothing but sex, dating, relationships, porn, masturbation, and so on. One of these retreats ended with a student-parent ceremony that included me signing a purity pledge that hung on a wall in my bedroom until I moved out for college. My parents gave me a purity ring at this ceremony, which I wore every day for years. (For a while I wore it on my left-hand ring finger, but I switched it to my right hand after getting too many weird looks and questions from friends, teachers, and coworkers. A couple years into college, the ring broke in half. I tried not to read too much into this.)

Some millennials look back with not much more than an amused eye roll when they think about purity pledges and '90s-era Christian music. Many don't feel they were harmed or malformed by this culture. I don't mean to paint an entire generation of Christians with broad brush strokes, but the neutral-to-positive experiences of some do not invalidate the negative experience of others (and vice versa). I'll just speak for myself: it's possible there are positive consequences of purity culture that I'm not aware of or don't fully appreciate. If I'm honest, my experiences in purity culture often feel like scars rather than blessings.

But purity rhetoric wasn't the only cultural challenge Christian millennials faced with regard to our sexuality. The arrival of the smartphone and high-speed internet combined to make pornography far more accessible than ever before. Most young men I knew both in the church and outside of it confessed, if pressed, to watching porn. For Christian guys, this was a constant weight of shame added to the obsessive messaging and pressures we received from purity culture.

LGBTQ+ millennials were also becoming increasingly open about their experiences. This created another layer of difficulty and confusion for Christian teens whose purity culture resources either didn't mention non-heterosexual experiences at all or responded to them with simplistic and dehumanizing solutions. "Pray the gay away" and "Adam and Eve, not Adam and Steve" were regular Christian tropes of my teen years. The practice of reparative therapy was common, wherein same-sex-attracted teens or adults were subjected to dehumanizing treatment with the express intent to "convert" them to heterosexual desire. Perhaps unsurprisingly, Christians did precious little during this time to counter the cultural tendencies of dehumanization endured by LGBTQ+ teens and adults.

While not on the same scale as the sexual revolution itself, the Purity Movement mixed with other cultural forces to create a cocktail of tension and confusion for many Christian teens. Even now in our late twenties, thirties, and early forties, the sons and daughters of purity culture are peeling back the layers of what it all meant for us. As one man I spoke to put it, "I feel like I've had to completely relearn my sexuality as an adult and unlearn so much of what evangelicalism taught me, not just about sex, but also about myself." In chapter two, I'll begin to unpack what it is about purity culture that many in my generation have found unhelpful in retrospect.

Gen Z—New challenges, no vision. The pace of social change in our culture is rapid—even disorienting. The newest generation of young people, Gen Z, faces its own unique challenges. The sexualization of popular culture continues unabated. What has changed is that teen pregnancy has dropped in recent years in America. Some argue this is a function of better sex education or access to contraception. It may simply be because teens are having less sex.[10] Does this signal that society has taken a turn toward traditional sexual values? Not exactly.

Mental health has replaced drugs, drunk driving, and teen pregnancy as the great challenge faced by the emerging generation. Teen use of antidepressants was steadily increasing in the years before Covid-19,[11] and difficulty attaining these prescriptions during lockdowns—combined with the stress and strain of remote learning—may have contributed to a further spike in teen mental health issues during the pandemic.[12] A larger-than-ever percentage of young people's social lives takes place online, a trend that the pandemic only accelerated. When I was growing up, social media was an online supplement to in-person gatherings. Today, the online world is often the locus of social interactions for young people. These and other trends have radically altered and complicated the sexual landscape of American teenagers. Social media platforms are sexualized and eroticized in a disembodied mode. Algorithms designed to prey on the curiosities of children and adults serve up whatever type of sexualized content captures one's attention. For adults, online dating is now the norm, but most people don't enjoy using these apps.[13] The church and Christians should have wisdom to offer about these new sexual practices, but the rhetoric of "saving yourself" for marriage seems less and less relevant to the challenges faced by young people today.

Moreover, Gen Zers (and millennials) have increasingly adopted the new, liberated consensus on human sexuality. This consensus prioritizes authenticity, consent, and personal expression. The Purity Movement's messages about sexual restraint before marriage and sexual freedom within heterosexual marriage ring hollow to a generation that rejects traditional categories.[14]

WHERE ARE WE NOW?

The narrative I've traced in this chapter is admittedly selective, representing one slice of a complex cultural story.[15] While it may be oversimplifying to describe these patterns in generational terms, such generalizations can sometimes be helpful for seeing the big picture. Older Christians who lived through the sexual revolution reared their children on an abstinence-focused, hetero-normative, patriarchal ethic. Now, many millennial children of the Purity Movement have rejected cultural and sexual ethics they grew up with.

The jig is up, as far as millennials and Gen Zers are concerned. The church has too often become a place of hate, sexual re-pression, false promises, and, worst of all, abuse. These people are either leaving behind traditional modes of Christian spiritu-ality or rejecting the faith altogether. Younger adults who grew up in the church are asking hard questions—questions that older generations of Christians seem unwilling to face: Is there any connection between purity culture and the broken masculinity that plagues the church? Why do so many people carry scars from purity teaching? Is this simply another generational in-stance of youthful angst? Rebelliousness? Or are the messages of purity culture harmful in themselves?

Was purity culture the faithful return to biblical sexuality that many Christian leaders made it out to be? Is it possible that the central tenets of purity culture are incompatible with the faith that Christians profess in an embodied, crucified, and resurrected Savior? Maybe, viewed from a certain perspective, purity culture never had any business calling itself a Christian movement in the first place.

TWO

THE "GREAT SEX" PROSPERITY GOSPEL

AND OTHER LIES OF THE PURITY MOVEMENT

I THOUGHT A LOT AS A TEENAGER about the refrain of Song of Songs: do not awaken love before its time. It felt like the biblical author knew there was something in me that refused to stay asleep. I longed for companionship, but my most constant companions were guilt and shame. The books I read, the conversations with my parents, and the youth group messages were clear: dire consequences would come if I woke love too early. To varying degrees, authority figures promised me blessing for obedience, including a safe and secure marriage with a heightened experience of pleasure and intimacy. Faithful obedience would guarantee freedom from shame. In this ideal world, I wouldn't make any sexual mistakes, so there wouldn't be anything for me to regret.

The promise of blessing and freedom wasn't enough. I couldn't keep my body under control; the longings, desires, and curiosities of my adolescent self would not stay asleep. And it wasn't just the wholesome future joys of marital intimacy that stirred me. The taboo things outside of "God's beautiful design for sex in marriage"—what I saw in movies, pornography, or heard about from friends—also awakened my curiosity. James Nelson describes this type of experience well: "Those moments of sexual fantasy which come unbidden and which both delight and disturb you."[1]

The destructive power of my sexuality demanded that it stay fully locked up. This meant no sex, except with your spouse, and only after your wedding. But it was considered especially pure and wise to maintain even stricter boundaries. Be wary of cuddling, kissing (particularly making out), spending time alone together, praying together, holding hands, and dancing. Keep it *all* under wraps and you'll increase your chances of making it to marriage with your purity intact. Though my mind assented to purity culture's logic, my adolescent body wasn't so sure. And because I couldn't keep my body asleep, I hated my body.

Late in college, I had a conversation with a coworker, Jim, that has always stuck with me. Jim and I were the only staff on the floor of the restaurant where we worked. It was an especially slow afternoon, which left us to make that unique type of workplace small talk as we waited for the shift to end. We had worked together for a couple years, and Jim knew I was studying at the Moody Bible Institute, a few blocks north of the restaurant.

After a silence Jim asked me, "Why are Christians so obsessed with sex?"

I was caught off guard. "What do you mean?"

"I mean you guys with this whole wait until marriage thing? Fighting against gay people getting married. Judging everybody who's having sex."

I hesitated as I gathered my thoughts. "I guess Christians just believe that God has a design and purpose for sex. And that living according to God's design leads to blessing and flourishing."

"That's fine for you guys, but why not just leave gay people alone? Why do you feel like you need to dictate what everyone else does? I mean, if you and your girlfriend don't want to have sex until you're married, good for you. But I feel like all Christians talk about is who should and shouldn't be having sex."

"Well, sex is a powerful thing, and I think we're just trying to advocate for what we think the truth is."

"How would you know sex is powerful if you've never experienced it?"

Now I was embarrassed. I certainly wasn't going to talk to Jim about the off and on battle I was waging against my consistent urges to look at pornography. The power of sex through pornography felt undeniable to me. I regularly felt unable to resist, despite my best efforts in prayer, accountability, and Scripture memory.

I tried to redirect. "Wouldn't you say the culture in general is obsessed with sex?"

Without hesitating, Jim said, "Well sure, in a way. But not the way Christians are. Hooking up with girls is something I like doing, but it's not something I think about all the time. Christians are the ones who seem weirdly obsessed with sex to me. So obsessed that they're always talking to other people about how they shouldn't be having it."

I thought a lot about this conversation in the weeks that followed. I had grown up in the church being taught that it was the world that was preoccupied with sex and sexuality. But what about Jim's read on Christians? Is it true that Christians are weirdly obsessed with sex? Have we been so busy pointing out the speck in the culture's eye that we've neglected the log in our own?[2]

TESTING OUR PURITY

In chapter one, I summarized the historical roots of purity culture. Now, we will look more closely at its messaging and rhetoric, particularly what I've come to see as its negative, dangerous, and damaging aspects.

I've had a lot of help in thinking this through. Many books have already been written critiquing purity culture. On the more conservative side we find Rachel Joy Welcher's *Talking Back to Purity Culture* (2019) and Sheila Gregoire's *The Great Sex Rescue* (2021) and *The Good Guy's Guide to Great Sex* (2022). Heading toward the more progressive end of the spectrum we find Linda Kay Klein's *Pure* (2018), Emily Joy Allison's *#ChurchToo* (2021), and Nadia Bolz-Weber's *Shameless* (2019). I've already mentioned academic and historical approaches to these topics, including the work of Kristin Kobes Du Mez and Sara Moslener. I commend the work of these women and encourage Christians, especially Christian leaders, to grapple with these books and their ideas. I don't always ascribe to their same conclusions, but I have been helped and challenged by every one of them, and have learned much from their research, insight, and courage.

The sheer volume of books published on purity culture raises the question, Why has this subcultural movement been subject to so much critique? And why was the Purity Movement so influential in the first place? Its rhetoric and messaging were compelling to church leaders, parents, and even teens. But the wisdom of the movement has not held up well to history in subsequent years. Why is this?

We read in the book of Proverbs, "There is a way that appears to be right, but in the end it leads to death" (Prov 14:12). In the history of the church, heresy has rarely taken the form of an outright contradiction to Christian teaching. More often it appears as a slight bending or twisting of the truth that nonetheless has serious theological or social implications. This is also the case with purity culture. Unhelpful messages appear alongside what I imagine even purity culture's harshest critics would agree is reasonable teaching about sex, love, and relationships. But the presence of some potentially helpful advice does not mean the moral or theological substructure of the movement was sound. To demonstrate this, we'll examine seven of purity culture's messages.

MESSAGE #1: BODIES ARE EVIL, SEX IS BAD

There is a contradiction at the heart of purity culture. On the one hand, we heard teaching that emphasized the goodness and beauty of sex. Sex was often celebrated as a gift from God. On the other hand, we were regularly warned about the dangers of sex, and some aspects of human sexuality were either never addressed directly or done so only in hurried and hushed tones. In another contradiction, bodies, particularly female bodies, were spoken of as beautiful and captivating creations, the crown jewel of the goodness and splendor of the world. At the same time, bodies were said to be dangerous, the cause of all our dark desires and sexual compulsions.

So which is it? Is sex a gift or a necessary evil? Are bodies good or destructive?

The book of Genesis teaches that the world God made is good. This includes our bodies and sexuality. But the forces of death, darkness, guilt, and shame—what many Christians call Satan and demons—hate God and his creation. They are intent on the death of humankind. The powers of death hate human bodies. They hate female bodies. They hate male bodies. They hate your sexuality and the life, vitality, and communion it brings to the world.[3]

In the Christian faith there is theological tension between created goodness and fallenness. All aspects of creation have been compromised by the dehumanizing force called sin, but the presence of sin and death do not erase the inherent goodness of embodied sexuality. Purity culture didn't always navigate this tension well. It taught sex was good as long as you waited for marriage. Bodies were good as long as they weren't experiencing sinful sexual desire or causing someone else to lust. Messages about the created goodness of sex often got lost in the warnings about the dangers of sexual immorality.

Because of this, body hatred thrives in purity culture. And the hatred of human bodies is not from God; it's from the devil. In this sense, purity culture isn't simply an extreme version of historic Christian sexual ethics. It is a perversion of Christian sexual ethics. It's not too Christian. It isn't Christian enough. Its messaging led many in my generation to feel that their bodies, sexuality, and sexual desires were helplessly and hopelessly evil. This is a direct, unbiblical contradiction to the Creator God's declaration that bodies are "very good" (Gen 1:31).

MESSAGE #2: YOUR BEST SEX LATER

Some of the most prominent Christian preachers in America regularly appeal to their audience's desires for wealth, health, and career success. Common among these teaching ministries is the promise that God will honor your "seed of faith" with an outpouring of future blessing. The implication is that if someone makes a financial donation to a church or ministry, that person can expect a future financial, health, or career blessing from God.

Conservative Christians often critique this teaching from the likes of Joel Osteen or Kenneth Copeland, calling it the "prosperity gospel." I believe the critics are right in doing so. This "gospel" is theologically incomplete and dangerous. Such teaching causes harm, not just by robbing people of their money, but by compromising people's view of God, shaming them for their lack of faith when the promised blessings don't come.

In a 2019 article, Katelyn Beaty wrote, "It is ironic that Christians who denounce the prosperity gospel have in recent years touted its sexier, if subtler form: the sexual prosperity gospel." This sexy false gospel "holds that God will reward premarital chastity with a good Christian spouse, great sex, perpetual marital fulfillment. . . . God wants to give you a hot spouse and a great sex life, as long as you wait."[4]

The theology that promises a life of marital sexual bliss is almost identical to the logic of the prosperity gospel. Instead of promising a hundredfold return on a financial donation, purity culture promised young people a return on their sexual down payment. Sex was used to sell abstinence.[5] These messages aimed especially at boys, capitalizing on a stereotype that teenage males only think about one thing. Promise them lots of great sex, and you'll get teen boys' attention.

But this promise simply isn't true. Yes, some who grew up hearing these messages did go on to have joy-filled and satisfying sexual relationships with their future spouses. But even these people, I imagine, would laugh thinking back at the hot and frequent marital sex they may have imagined when they were teenagers. More to the point, many who *did* follow the laws of purity culture never saw this sexual blessing materialize. Instead, they were left with frustration and disappointment.

Sexual frustration and disappointment take many forms. They may look like ongoing loneliness as the season of singleness extends longer than you hoped or expected. They may look like finding yourself single again after your first marriage falls apart. They may look like struggling to even find the opposite sex appealing as you constantly redirect your family's questions about when you'll start dating. They may look like an ongoing experience of infertility, or a struggle to even enjoy sex with your spouse.

For me, sexual frustration has looked like lying awake more nights than I can count, feeling hopeless and lonely as the love of my life sleeps next to me. I'm agonizing over the fact that my wife does not desire me sexually. She can hardly connect with her sexuality at all. For me, sexual disappointment has looked like dozens of hours spent in therapy, counselors assuring me that my wife's trauma triggers have nothing to do with me.

My experience of sexuality has not felt like God's blessing. Instead, if I'm honest, it has felt like a curse. I, like many others, tried my hardest to follow the rules. Shelby and I were both virgins on our wedding night, and our marriage has been characterized by ongoing sexual frustration, loneliness, and pain.

MESSAGE #3: SEXUAL CERTAINTY IN AN UNCERTAIN WORLD

Being a teenager is delicate business. Bodies change quickly. Hormones rage. Relationships are high stakes and often cutthroat and cruel. Insecurity abounds. The future can seem exciting and terrifying all at once. Pressure from family, teachers, friends, and church pull in multiple, often conflicting directions. First-in-a-lifetime experiences come regularly. New heights of emotion, both positive and negative, are common.

Teenagers and young people experience some of the deepest longings in life, and sexuality is often an especially confusing and uncertain aspect of these years. Am I desirable? Will anyone ever love me in this way? Will my body always look like this? What if I'm alone forever? Purity teaching filled this space by trying to provide a type of certainty. Books, parents, and pastors often assured young people that some behaviors would lead to specific favorable or unfavorable outcomes. Even when the overstated language of "I promise" wasn't used, implied guarantees and assurances were powerful for teenagers plagued by uncertainty.

"I read *I Kissed Dating Goodbye* in high school," said Tony, one of the men I interviewed for this book. "There was this allure of certainty. Evangelicalism sets it up as this idea of 'Do it this way and it'll pay off.' I wanted to do this right. If I did it right, I thought I could avoid harm. And avoid pain and suffering."

Fifteen years later, Tony views sexuality and marriage differently. He is a survivor of church-based sexual abuse, and what's perhaps most tragic about his experience is that he was being taken advantage of by an older man around the same time he was exposed to the promises and assurances of purity culture. His interactions with his abuser and the high-stakes rhetoric of purity culture combined to create a torturous experience of shame around romance and sexuality.

Tony no longer identifies as a Christian, and now he's not sure he wants to get married at all. "All that certainty stuff is a façade. I saw four of my closest friends get divorced in 2019. At thirty years old, I'm still a virgin—and I don't want to be. I need to inch my way into enjoying and celebrating desire." When he and I spoke for this book, he was in a long-term dating relationship. He'd like to be able to connect physically with his partner, but his body won't let him—despite the fact he no longer subscribes to the no-sex-before-marriage purity ideal. It's not that he thinks it's wrong to have sex. It's that he cannot passionately kiss his girlfriend without his body going into panic mode.

"The way we're taught ingrains itself in our biology," Tony told me. "Reversing that is no simple task. I'm lucky enough to have income where I can go to therapy and dig into all this at a pretty intense level. A lot of people don't have that."

Pastors, parents, and authors promised too much. There is no certainty in this life, as much as we might wish for it. As much as we may wish that there was a way to guarantee future outcomes for our career, marriage, or finances, this is not how the world works. It's not how life works—even life with God.

MESSAGE #4: SEXUAL SIN ALWAYS HAS CLEAR CONSEQUENCES

One of my pastors growing up often repeated the axiom, "Choose to sin, choose to suffer." While this statement is proverbially true, it is not always the whole picture of life in this world. Some sexual choices may lead directly or indirectly to suffering, but choosing to abstain from sex altogether does not shield us from all sexual suffering—just ask a victim of sexual assault or childhood sexual abuse.

The emphasis on blessings and consequences in purity culture has led some to ask what they did wrong to deserve their sexual suffering. Was I abused and assaulted because I dressed immodestly? Is God punishing me for having sex with my girlfriend in high school? If I had watched less porn when I was younger would I be married now? If I had been more willing to surrender my sexuality to God in college, would I have children already? Am I reaping the consequences for masturbating and lusting after women or men?

Jesus' disciples once asked a similar question: "Who sinned, this man or his parents, that he was born blind?" Jesus responded, "Neither this man nor his parents sinned" (Jn 9:2-4). Jesus rejects the one-to-one connection between someone's sin and their future suffering. Yes, actions have consequences, but God does not delight in punishing us for making mistakes or being sexual creatures. Some people who have sex with someone they aren't married to may see clear and negative consequences for that choice; others may not. While some see clear blessing for their discipline and self-control; others may not.

I'm not making a specific argument about sexual ethics, pre-marital or otherwise. I'm seeking to make a point about who God is and how he relates to fallen humans. Again, it is true that you reap what you sow (Gal 6:7), but even this biblical principle should never be taken to imply certain choices obligate God to reward or punish in specific ways. Nor does it imply that obedience *always* leads to tangible blessing and sin *always* leads to future suffering. On the contrary, in the Scriptures, it is often the wicked who prosper and the righteous who suffer—just read the book of Job.

MESSAGE #5: SEX AT THE CENTER

A cultural innovation of the sexual revolution was the insistence that sex didn't have to be a big deal. Sex, it's been argued, is merely a bodily function, a recreational activity that shouldn't be freighted with all the added weight of religious conviction or rules. Liberated sexuality meant consenting adults should be able to engage in casual sex without judgment or risk. Feminist philosopher and author Amia Srinivasan describes this attitude shift well: "Since the 1980s . . . sex is no longer morally problematic or unproblematic: it is instead merely wanted or unwanted. In this sense, the norms of sex are like the norms of capitalist free exchange. What matters is . . . that both buyer and seller have agreed to the transfer."[6]

Purity culture reacted to this anti-authoritarian approach by doubling down on the importance of sex and insisting it is a very big deal and that God's authority through Scripture dictates clear rules and consequences for sexual sin. However, this well-intentioned focus on sexuality evolved into something else. Sex, abstinence, and purity became the be-all and end-all of Christian teenage discipleship. The message many of us received was that this was the battle on which our soul would be lost or won.

Bobby, one of the men I interviewed for this book, described joining a youth ministry as a high school student. "I was drawn in by the love of God. But from a few months in it seemed like the primary goal was to stop masturbating, and stop looking at porn, and get a wife. It's so weird that there's a hyperfixation on sexuality and it's also the one thing that we should never do." Julie, a woman I interviewed, recalled talking about sexual purity "at least monthly," plus going to the annual True Love Waits conference.

In purity culture, sexual sins such as viewing pornography were seen as the most dangerous and threatening. Sociologist Samuel Perry summarizes this well:

> Protestants largely subscribe to sexual exceptionalism, counting sexual sin as the most corrupting and damnable of all sins. Consequently, pornography use—not anger, greed, selfishness, racism, pride, or envy—often becomes a proxy for measuring the quality of a believer's spiritual life. In other words, as one's battle with lust goes, so goes their relationship with God and their perceived worth as a Christian.[7]

Being right with God in your sexuality meant everything was right. Falling into sexual sin meant everything was wrong.

This sexual exceptionalism made me think it was a serious sin when, in seventh grade, my mutual crush and I decided to label our relationship as "going out." Sexual exceptionalism meant my first kiss, at fourteen, was an occasion for deep shame, a palpable sense

I had let down my parents, my future wife, and God. Sexual exceptionalism meant my ongoing struggle against pornography suggested that my Christian faith was a farce, that I had committed the worst imaginable type of offense.

The half-truth here is that sexuality is indeed a powerful aspect of the human experience. Our sexual choices have real implications for our lives, including our spiritual lives. The warnings older adults gave were not hollow. Serious, life-altering consequences can accompany shortsighted and foolish youthful decisions about when, how, and whom you engage sexually. But the excessive airtime given to avoiding sexual sin in purity culture implied that staying sexually pure was the primary calling of Christian discipleship.

Sexuality is one aspect of our life, not the totality of it. No teenager, Christian or otherwise, should feel that their worth before God, their parents, or their spouse is contingent on whether they had sex before marriage. This type of performative righteousness is contrary to the gospel. When Christian parents and leaders implied as much, they were working counter to God's grace in teenagers' lives, aligning themselves with the Great Accuser (Rev 12:10) who wants us to doubt God's love for us.

Yes, sex is important, but where this thinking goes awry is when we shift from *sex is important* to *sex is everything*. In more recent years, the sex-is-no-big-deal approach of the sexual revolution has been supplemented with the view that sex is a core expression of our identity. Somehow, sex is nothing and everything at the same time. The perhaps unanticipated point of agreement that has emerged between cultural conservatives and progressives is this: sexual identity and what we choose to do with our sexual bodies is a central aspect of what it means to be human. As Christine Emba writes, "Whether one is having sex or refraining from it, either way, sex is meaningful. It cannot be easily contained and should not be downplayed. We cannot make it small."[8] Yes, sex is a big deal. Purity culture got that much right. But sex isn't everything.

MESSAGE #6: SINGLENESS IS SUBHUMAN
(AND ONLY TEMPORARY)

In many Christian contexts, marriage was (and is) understood as an eventuality rather than a possibility. A happy and prosperous marriage is described as the endgame of young Christians' hopes and dreams for their life. They are told to live faithfully in the present, not indulging in sexual sin, and eventually God will reward them with the sexual and relational fulfillment they desire in marriage. But is this a sound biblical claim? You'd be hard pressed to find direct scriptural support of the notion that God promises sexual, marital fulfillment to those who obey his commands.

Some Christians criticize LGBTQ+ activists for claiming a right to marriage. Someone's desire for a certain type of relationship doesn't mean they should have a legal or moral right to it, or so the argument goes. Ironically, Christians leveling these critiques have often adopted a similar logic for straight, cisgendered sexual fulfillment. Bridget Eileen Rivera explains this cruel irony in the way evangelical Christians often speak about sex.[9] On the one hand, they suggest that forced celibacy is unreasonable and unnatural for sexually frustrated straight young men. Marriage is reduced to a God-given outlet for sexual desire and women reduced to objects for the fulfillment of men's sexual needs. On the other hand, when speaking to queer Christians, there is no "provision" for their desire; lifelong celibacy is God's righteous requirement. How is it that we think of chaste living as a cruel and borderline impossible expectation for one group of Christians while *requiring* it of another group? Rivera summarizes: "Evangelical Christians promote a narrative about human sexuality that contradicts the expectations placed on queer people. The message that LGBTQ+ people internalize is that God promises wonderful things in exchange for Christian obedience—but only if you're straight."[10] I'd add, the message that straight young men internalize is that sexual fulfillment in marriage is their God-given right.

Christians who hold to a traditional view of gay relationships should ask themselves whether straight young men are likewise expected to live sexually responsible and self-controlled lives, even for extended or indefinite singleness. Are we consistent in the way we speak about sexual desire and fulfillment? The bar is often set far lower for straight young men than it is for other Christians. Marriage, not sexual maturity, is presented as the endgame of this aspect of Christian discipleship. If heterosexual marriage is the destination, unmarried people haven't arrived. Marriage is presented as a type of salvation—from loneliness, sexual sin, and a lack of wholeness.[11] But for many, it doesn't seem like this salvation is coming any time soon, or even at all.

Not everyone gets married, and when marriage is described as God's reward for sexual abstinence, those who remain single become second-class citizens in God's kingdom. This is one piece in a larger system of idolatry toward the nuclear family. Yes, God cares about marriage, children, and sex. But he also wants to bless and care for widows and orphans, singles, and members of sexual minority groups.

MESSAGE #7: BOYS ARE DANGEROUS (AND SO ARE GIRLS)

The youth group events and summer camps I attended in high school had strict "no two-piece" policies for girls. Girls who did happen to bring a two-piece swimsuit (whether out of ignorance or rebellion against these rules) were required to wear a T-shirt over their suit for games and swimming. The implicit message within this policy is that girls' and young women's bodies are dangerous.

Boys and girls were often warned about each other in purity culture. These messages went something like this: "Girls, don't hug boys straight on because the feeling of your breasts against his body will cause him to think sexual thoughts about you. It's unkind and inconsiderate to hug boys or wear form-fitting clothing. You don't want to attract the wrong type of attention." Or "Boys, be careful of girls who show romantic interest in you or are too physically affectionate. At any time, they could use the power of their body against you and cause you to compromise your future marriage and obedience to God. If they do this, you would certainly be unable to resist."

These messages culminate in a culture of mistrust and fear. Christian teens were encouraged to view sexuality only as a weapon to be guarded against. Is this the message we want adolescents carrying with them into adulthood? That men are inherently dangerous? That women are inherently dangerous? That being in relational proximity to members of the opposite sex is not worth the risk?

Yes, sin and sexual brokenness are real. But teaching men and women to be afraid of each other because of their gender is not a recipe for authentic, life-giving community. Many who received this type of teaching were left feeling that their *bodies* were bad and dangerous. This is, again, not a Christian way of thinking about bodies, and it's not difficult to see how people receiving these messages might struggle with physical intimacy later in life.

SEXUAL IDOLATRY AND SHAME

Instead of redirecting young people away from the worship of sex, purity culture rhetoric used the Christian God as a means to the true end that many teenagers were interested in: relational security and mind-blowing sex. Just as our adherence to the prosperity gospel shows we are worshiping money rather than God, our adherence to the sexual prosperity gospel shows us to be worshippers of sex rather than Jesus Christ.

Idols lie. And they inevitably disappoint and let us down. We must face the reality that many of these promises are simply not true. Even those who followed the rules often find their marriages plagued with difficulty and sexual dysfunction. To those who feel burned or let down by purity culture, know this: it's not your fault.

This is the fault of a broken system and heretical theology, a church culture that too often used the Lord's name in vain, making him a magic genie who could guarantee what we really wanted—great sex. Though it often masqueraded as biblical wisdom, purity culture's shame-fueled approach and heretical prosperity teaching are contrary to the gospel of Jesus Christ—and shame sticks. This feeling is common to many who grew up in this movement, but it takes various forms: Shame about what I've done. Shame about what's been done to me. Shame about what I've thought about doing. Shame about what I've seen or where I've been. Shame about what I've found exciting. Shame about what I've found unexciting. Shame about what I've desired, who I've desired. Shame about what I am. Shame about who I am.

The shame boys and men experience in purity culture is different from that experienced by girls and women, but it is shame all the same. A vision of sexuality rooted in guilt and shame is not a Christian vision of sexuality. Purity culture has badly hurt many women, *and* it has also led to great harm for men. It has left an entire generation of Christian men with a skewed vision of who they are as sexual beings created in God's image. Rather than challenge perspectives that saw men as out-of-control sexual "animals," the messages many men (and women) got in church confirmed and reinforced the worst cultural stereotypes about male sexuality. Purity culture didn't invent toxic masculinity, but many toxic and dehumanizing tendencies have found their way into our churches through its messages. This connection between purity culture and toxic dehumanization will be our topic for chapters three and four.

THREE

THE DEHUMANIZATION OF MEN

WHAT IS TOXIC MASCULINITY
AND WHERE DO WE SEE IT IN THE CHURCH?

THE PROBLEM OF TOXIC MASCULINITY is much bigger than contemporary expressions of Christian faith. Mistreatment of women and men's routine dehumanization of others have been features of every culture in human history.[1] If Christianity ceased to exist tomorrow, toxic masculinity would remain. The problem is not, in its essence, a Christian problem. Rather, it is a problem of human nature.

Part of the issue stems from the biological differences between male and female bodies. Generally speaking, adult male bodies have a raw advantage of physical size and strength when compared to female bodies. We might call this pattern "embodied male advantage," and it is, like it or not, a fact of nature. This doesn't mean that male bodies are better for performing *all* physical tasks, or that male embodiment is somehow superior to female embodiment, but it should not be controversial to say there are biological patterns of difference.

Differences in physical strength matter a lot when it comes to injustice.[2] For instance, my five-year-old daughter has a clear embodied physical advantage over my three-year-old son. She often uses this advantage to create an unjust system of play. She's bigger, stronger, and more practiced in appealing to the authority structure of the home (her parents). The fact that she's a girl and he's a boy is irrelevant. If she chooses, she can push him around, grab toys out of his hand, and assert her will over his.

Something similar has happened with men and women in human society. Embodied male advantage gives men power to pursue their own selfish ends if they so choose. They can assert their will on both individual women and women as a group. These physical advantages have formed the foundation for what is sometimes called *male privilege*. Not every aspect of male privilege is about physical strength, but that strength formed its starting point. Male embodied advantage leads to male privilege.

Is this embodied advantage itself wrong or evil? Is it sinful to be a man or to have a male body? Does male advantage necessarily turn into toxic masculinity? The answer to all three of these questions is no.

The expression of maleness becomes toxic when men leverage their embodied advantage to harm and dehumanize others. Oxford Dictionaries Online gives the following definition for toxic masculinity: "A set of attitudes and ways of behaving stereotypically associated with or expected of men, regarded as having a negative impact on men and on society as a whole."[3] I listed some of these attitudes and behaviors in the introduction: emotional repression, entitlement, aggression, and so on. What people associate with toxic masculinity can be largely summed up in a single word: *dehumanization*.

Here is my working definition: *toxic masculinity is a way of thinking, living, and acting as a male that dehumanizes self and others.* To put it another way, toxic masculinity involves men leveraging embodied male advantage for selfish ends, thus dehumanizing others and men themselves.

Though we might want to, we can't wish away women's physical disadvantages. Instead, we should acknowledge the differences between male and female bodies and think together about how to build a safe and equitable society (and church) where both men and women can flourish. When men allow their embodied advantage to morph into dehumanizing attitudes and behaviors, they become complicit in the fracturing of the world and society. Christians call this breaking of the world *sin*. Thus, for Christians, a good way to understand toxic masculinity is, simply, the distinct way that sin has broken and fractured the expression of male embodiment.

Maybe you believe Christianity is oppressive, patriarchal, and violent at its core. Maybe you believe toxic masculinity cannot be separated from the Christian faith. I understand why you might. Too often Christians are at the center of abuse scandals. Too often professing Christians defend and protect abusers, not the abused. Even worse, "Christian" abusers use their spiritual influence as a weapon against their victims. In one sense, the Christian faith cannot be separated from the long history of misogyny, including ongoing, even egregious examples. In another sense, I believe oppression and violence against women is contrary to the true spirit of the Christian faith. Christians should both address the manifestations of toxic masculinity in our own communities and oppose toxic masculinity in broader society. The church should be a place of healing and resurrection, not abuse and dehumanization.

CORRECTING THE MALE PERSPECTIVE

One central privilege resulting from male embodied advantage is the fact that society as a whole is structured in a way that skews toward stereotypically male ways of viewing the world. This goes beyond biological sex, and some may specify further that the dominant perspective is a white, cis-gendered, able-bodied, heterosexual male with a good education and financial stability. I'm focusing on maleness in this book, but I want to acknowledge that power and dehumanization intersect with a variety of factors. We all have our own biases and perspectives. This can tend toward an implicit belief that those who view and experience the world differently than we do aren't seeing the world as they should.

Default male perspective is present throughout our society. For instance, "male gaze" storytelling refers to the tendency for cinematographers, animators, and designers to sexualize female bodies in media. This affects everything from camera angles to casting to costume design to acting direction.[4]

American evangelicalism has its own male gaze—the lens through which Christian teachers speak about women's bodies, sex, and the rules around public interactions. In fact, a reason purity culture's most outspoken critics are female is that purity culture messaging is run through with a male perspective. Men may be less inclined to see problems with the movement because purity culture reinforces their assumptions about the world. For instance, purity culture regulates women's clothing but says comparatively little about ways men dress or act that may be unhelpful or harmful to women. Purity culture majors on a wife's sexual duty to her husband but says comparatively little about a husband's responsibility to love and serve his wife sexually. Purity culture prioritizes the integrity of male leaders in the church while often ignoring the way rules about male-female relationships make women in the congregation feel marginalized or humiliated.

To stem the tide of abuse in the church, we must account for and correct this skewed male perspective. Women (and children!) regularly experience injustice in our communities. The church sets the standards for men far too low, treating them more like animals than responsible moral agents. If a broken vision of masculinity were the roots of a tree, the dehumanization of women would be the fruit growing on its branches, which is why women, by and large, have been the first to call on the church (and the culture) to correct these injustices. But the fault remains with men, and thus correcting the problem must start with men.

TO BE MALE IS TO BE HYPERSEXUAL
(OR, THE SUBHUMAN MALE MIND)

In an oft-quoted section of Arterburn and Stoeker's *Every Man's Battle*, they claim that men are more inclined toward sexual sin "naturally—simply by being male."[5] Whatever the authors' intention, the teaching that hyperactive and out-of-control sexual desire is an unavoidable part of being male is one of the most damaging messages of purity culture.

Yes, the stereotype of teenage boys' rampant fantasy lives and frequent habit of masturbating exists for a reason. Many young men experience sexual arousal at the slightest provocation—or even no discernible provocation. It may seem like all it takes is a strong gust of wind. But, even if many young men experience desires that feel difficult to control, maleness should not be defined by its sexual urges. The stereotype is just that: a stereotype. Not every teenage boy is obsessed with female bodies. Largely due to the influence of books like *Every Man's Battle* and *For Women Only*, extreme erotic interest in female bodies has become the measuring stick by which young boys in Christian culture gauge whether they or their peers are becoming real men.

But remember we're talking about teenagers. This hypersexualized masculinity is a common expression of an immature male sexuality. Is there anything wrong with being immature? In a sense, no. We expect children and young people to think and act immaturely. We also expect them to grow out of immaturity as they age. What about adult men? Inasmuch as we've accepted this adolescent male tendency as an inevitable part of being male, we've accommodated to grown men's ongoing sexual immaturity.

Purity culture dehumanizes women and girls by oversexualizing their bodies. It dehumanizes men and boys by oversexualizing their minds. It teaches that men, because they are men, view the world through an erotic lens. "Men are visual,"[6] and a man cannot be expected to resist the overwhelming physical response he experiences at the unwelcome thought, sight, or (heaven forbid) sexual advance of a woman who is not his wife. Here again, purity culture defines maleness in terms of rampant, untamable sexual desire.

I don't mean to deny the unique power of sexual temptation in many men's experiences of the world, but I sometimes wonder if we have given sexual sin more credit than it deserves. Yes, every aspect of our humanity, in mind, body, and soul, has been tainted by sin. But sometimes, when we're talking about men, it seems we think of their sexuality as especially or even hopelessly depraved. Are men more inclined toward sexual sin than greed, violence, idolatry, or dishonesty? When a man lies, steals, acts violently or manipulatively, we hold him morally responsible.[7] But for some categories of sexual misconduct (that is, sin), we act like a man couldn't be expected to do otherwise.

The rate at which men in the church struggle with sexual sin isn't simply a function of their maleness; it is a function of the way we teach men to think about themselves. This oversexualized view of the male mind has become a self-fulfilling prophecy. Instead, boys should be encouraged from a young age to view women as human beings, not sexual objects. Boys should be taught to dignify themselves as moral agents, not sex machines following their programming.

MEN OF DESIRE

The "sex machine" vision of masculinity plays off other Western male stereotypes. One such stereotype is that men are non-emotional, or at least less emotional than women. The sociological and historical reasons for this are beyond the scope of this book, but is there anything inherently male about emotional stoicism? Many of our most cherished artists and fictional characters are men who are in touch with their emotions. What would we say about Lin Manuel Miranda's Alexander Hamilton? Or William

Shakespeare's love sonnets? Are these men less manly for having feelings? What of the intimacy and expressions of love and affection between Frodo and Sam in *The Lord of the Rings*? Many heroes of the Christian faith were also emotional men. Martin Luther's emotional experiences were instrumental in the Protestant Reformation. Saint Augustine's *Confessions* is thoroughly emotional. King David passionately wrote about his love for God (Ps 63) and his confession of his sin (Ps 51). As one man I interviewed put it, "Yes, David was a warrior, but he didn't write *The Art of War*; he wrote the Psalms."

Despite this, men are not socialized to understand or articulate what they are feeling. This nonemotional masculine narrative extends into the Christian subculture's vision of male sexuality. Men, it is said, are preoccupied with physical or visual aspects of sex and eroticism. Women, it is said, are more interested in the emotional connection and relational aspects of sex. These, again, are stereotypes. Men are emotionally invested in sex and sexuality and plenty of women enjoy visual stimulation. The gravitational pull of pornography, for instance, involves emotions. Christian men who watch porn may say they do it because they find the female form alluring, but what many men don't understand is that porn is fulfilling an emotional need.

If you watch porn, ask yourself this: Why do you watch the type of porn you watch? What about these sexual interactions captivates you? What wound is this medicating? What unfulfilled spiritual, relational, and emotional wants are driving you?

Christian teaching sells men short on emotional complexity. There is much more to their desire for sex than the pursuit of visual stimulation or the physical release of an orgasm. If desire was just about orgasm, masturbation would be good enough. But most men would agree that their longing for sexual fulfillment and connection is not met by this act. Men don't simply want to orgasm, view female nudity, or have sex with wives who feel obligated to do so. Men want to feel desired. They want emotional connection, whether they realize it or can articulate it.

I've come to realize this in my own experience. About five years into our marriage, Shelby confessed to me that she rarely desires sex. Despite this, we had been having sex with some consistency throughout most of our marriage. Once I realized she was only being intimate out of obligation to serve my physical needs, the thought of continuing to have this type of sex lost its appeal. She had consistently made herself available, but once I knew it wasn't coming from her own desire, the spell was broken. I wanted to connect with my wife, but one-sided sex isn't connection. As Meg Ryan shows in *When Harry Met Sally*, women can be pretty good at faking it. Consider for a moment why women feel pressure to pretend they're enjoying sex when they're not. It's because both men and women intuit that one-sided sex isn't "real" sex, and it would hurt the man's feelings to know his partner isn't enjoying herself. But is simply appeasing the male ego the best way to address this common form of sexual dysfunction?

This brings up the important question of sexual consent. Shelby and I have talked about this at length as it relates to our relationship. She believes she always consented to having sex. I never forced her to do anything, but that doesn't mean our sexual relationship was healthy. In many relationships, cultural expectations create a system of pressure and coercion that can be difficult to detect. This is where sexual ethics that focus only on consent fall short.[8] Shelby was a consenting participant, but not because she desired sex herself. Both parties can consent to one-sided sex, but that should not be the bar set for a healthy relationship. Just because it's not rape doesn't mean it isn't dehumanizing.

In a sense, it was kind and caring for Shelby to have sex with me even when she didn't want to. She did it because she loves me. However, obligatory sex was hurting her. What seemed like a kindness to my body was an unkindness to hers. These days we are only intimate if Shelby really wants to. She initiates the majority of our sexual encounters, and, for now at least, this means we engage sexually far less than we did earlier in our marriage. On one hand, this is difficult for me. But I much prefer infrequent mutual connection to frequent one-sided sexual encounters. This is a more emotionally fulfilling—more human—way of relating. Men are human beings, not sex machines. It is important that we understand and acknowledge the way sex connects to a man's emotional needs and complexity as a person, not just his felt need for physical release.

Curt Thompson writes, "The beauty, energy, and vulnerability bound up and often expressed in our sexuality often points to something that is deeper and beyond sex itself."[9] He goes on,

> A critical element of our desire is that of being desired. We long to be infinitely desired, wanted by the other yet—and crucially—without being consumed by the other. Without being exploited. Without being ignored or imprisoned. This begins at birth and winds its way through all our relationships at every level of intimacy. . . . No matter how superficial or deep, this seminal drive for connection is preeminent.[10]

Sex connects to a much larger network of emotional and relational desires that form the heart of what makes human beings unique. Sadly, men are often told that their desire for sex is the most superficial and uncomplicated thing about them. Nothing could be further from the truth.

MODELS OF MALE SEXUALITY

Mel Gibson's *Braveheart* is sometimes referenced as a clear example of true masculinity. For all the courage and strength on display in Gibson's portrayal of William Wallace, something else comes through: sexual conquest. The film includes portrayals of not one but two of Wallace's sexual relationships, the second of which is with another man's wife. The film includes multiple scenes of women swooning at the thought of Wallace's warrior escapades. William Wallace was idolized in the white Christian subculture when I was a teen. I can't tell you how many guys claimed *Braveheart* as their favorite movie. Sexual conquest is characteristic of all manner of male heroes and role models—Han Solo, James Bond, Tony Stark, and, for an older generation, the many characters portrayed by John Wayne.

Even Prince Charming, whom many claim as the paragon of Western masculine virtue, isn't free from this trait. The rescue of the princess in a tower, the slaying of the dragon, and every other Western trope of masculine heroism often implies a type of sexual conquest. While the sexual subtext of fairy tales is not stated explicitly, the implication is that the knight's (violent) heroism gains him access to the sexual affections of the princess.

Maybe this strikes you as overly cynical, but the formative power of stories such as this should not be underestimated. Boys watching these stories come to see courage and heroism as a means to a romantic or sexual end. These narratives teach both boys and girls to think men are entitled to romantic or sexual attention if they act chivalrously. The reality is women don't always (or even usually) need men's help. But if they do, men should help simply because it's right, not because they'll be (sexually) rewarded for it.

The ministry of pastor Mark Driscoll adds another important wrinkle to this story. Young men who were adolescents during the height of purity culture (the early 2000s) emerged as adults at the height of Driscoll's influence (2010–2014). Both Driscoll's preaching and writing were characterized by a clear vision for masculinity, calling young men to grow up, get married, and provide financially for their families. This was a captivating vision for lots of men and boys, myself included. It should be acknowledged that the ministry of Mars Hill, Driscoll's church, saw many young men convert to faith and launch out of substance abuse and perpetual adolescence into stable careers and fatherhood. But Driscoll's brand of masculinity was stereotypically macho and muscular. More to the point, his teaching included edgy, even graphic, descriptions of sex. He described this domineering and hypersexual masculinity as biblical and exhorted young men in his church with angry rants and extended discussions of the wife's duty of marital relations with her husband.[11]

Finally, President Donald Trump, a man platformed and celebrated by many in the evangelical subculture, is a horrendous model of masculine sexuality. Trump has had multiple divorces and known encounters with prostitutes, as well as manifold credible allegations of sexual abuse and rape.[12] He makes dehumanizing remarks about women's appearances and boasted that his wealth and fame gave him unique power over women, so much so that he could "grab them by the pussy." It's troubling that such a person was ever viewed as a "real man" or a Christian hero. Christian boys and girls were paying attention when Trump was elevated to the nation's highest office—even as his sins against women were excused, tolerated, and dismissed as irrelevant by Christian leaders.

These role models have done little to challenge the cultural attitudes of male sexual entitlement, a central feature of toxic masculinity.

PERFORMING MASCULINITY

Every culture has its own definition of masculinity, an ideal to which men are encouraged to conform. Depending on who you ask, the American masculine ideal may include such values as strength, courage, financial independence, career success, sexual prowess, fatherhood—or even something as arbitrary as the ability to shoot a gun or chop down a tree. It's important to remember that these definitions are culturally situated and not all men will fit the narrative. Nathan Pyle writes, "Much of the work that has been done to define masculinity seeks to fit all men into the same rigid mold: wild, tough warriors who cannot be tamed."[13]

The Christian masculine ideal is in some ways distinct from that of the broader culture, but the pressure that Christian boys and men feel to conform is the same. For instance, many Christians view getting married as a graduation into manhood. Successfully wooing, dating, and marrying a woman is part of proving one's manhood, a framing especially common in Driscoll's teaching. If you couldn't or didn't care to do this, you weren't a real man.

In more ways than one, purity culture set out a masculine ideal that only worked for some men. To fit this ideal, your sexual attraction to women had to be intense enough to make you feel manly by cultural standards. At the same time, your ability to control your sexuality and desire had to be strong enough to effectively avoid lust and sexual sin. Holding these two standards in tension is difficult for many men—and impossible for men who aren't sexually attracted to women at all. Admitting you struggle to meet purity culture's standards amounts to admitting you fall outside of the Christian masculine ideal. My friend Chris put it this way: "Purity culture's ideals were so far from who I was and my lived experience that the only possible outcome was crippling guilt and shame."

Purity culture doesn't simply set a bar that's difficult to meet; it emasculates men who don't experience hyper-heterosexual desire. The heterosexual perspective assumed by purity culture's teaching leaves gay, asexual, or low-libido men wondering where they fit into the Christian narrative. Christian masculinity shouldn't exclude men who don't fit the hypersexual masculine norm.[14] It should grant all men agency, dignity, and full humanity as creatures made in the image of God. Christians should affirm all godly men who are filled with the fruit of the Spirit—even if they don't fit cultural norms of masculinity.

MEN WILL BE BOYS

The dehumanizing messages of purity culture are as pervasive as they are subtle. The church often manages to set both a pathetically low and impossibly high bar for masculine sexuality. It trains men to resist, flee, and medicate (through marital sex) their untamable boyish immaturity rather than grow beyond it. Boyish sexual behavior is too often normalized. We need to ask deeper questions about male sexuality than the simplistic approach offered by purity culture. When we neglect to give men resources and vision for mature masculine sexuality we should not be surprised when they continue to act like teenagers.

Thank God, many Christian men are better than purity culture makes them out to be; they don't embody this immature expression of sexuality. However, these messages about masculinity have made the subculture a haven for dehumanization. In these toxic environments, women are held responsible for men's sin and are disempowered, prevented from seeking their own good and flourishing. Women are regularly harmed in significant ways because of this masculine immaturity.

FOUR

THE DEHUMANIZATION OF WOMEN

HOW WOMEN ARE HARMED BY FRACTURED MASCULINITY

IN #CHURCHTOO: *How Purity Culture Upholds Abuse and How to Find Healing,* Emily Joy Allison tells her story of church-based sexual abuse. Allison and I grew up in similar church environments hearing similar messages about sexuality. We even went to the same Bible college. Her book is one of the more thoughtful, accessible, and compassionate critiques of purity culture I've read. I recommend it—not because I agree with everything she says, but because many of her critiques are weighty and important. Theological conservatives will find plenty to disagree with, but disagreement should not be an excuse to ignore her. As Allison herself puts it, "Evangelical Christians who are committed to purity culture show by their actions that they love their ideas about who God is and what God wants more than they love the actual people in front of them."[1] This is pretty damning. Do evangelicals have a reputation for a strict set of rules about sexual behavior? You bet. Do evangelicals have a reputation for believing, caring for, and advocating on behalf of victims of church-based sexual abuse? Not so much.

Allison was groomed in high school for a romantic relationship with a man almost twice her age. After convincing her that such a romance could be "God-honoring," they secretly began to spend more time alone together. When the relationship came to light, *she* was punished by her parents and forced to call and apologize to her abuser. Allison's story is heartbreaking.[2] I don't mean that in a patronizing way. I can see why she's mad as hell about all this. In reading her story, I was angry with the people who hurt her, her parents and friends who blamed her for her trauma. It was the same anger I felt when my wife and I learned that she, too, was a victim of church-based sexual abuse. It's the same anger I feel when other women I know and love dearly tell me their stories of abuse, and the calloused, even cruel, responses they too often heard from Christians. No one should be treated this way. The fact that abuse, retraumatization, gaslighting, and victim blaming happen so often in Christian communities makes me even more angry.

I still hold to a traditional sexual ethic, but it's not the most important thing about my Christian faith. It is, to me, a secondary issue. And I believe it should be. We need to be careful about how we equate a certain sexual ethic with the gospel itself.[3] We should also ask if we care more about our understanding of doctrinal purity or church attendance and budgets than we do about people's physical safety and the tangible suffering of women in our communities.

Some critics of purity culture, like Allison, have openly dedicated themselves to overturning traditional Christian views on human sexuality. Even if you disagree with her on this point, it would be a serious mistake to dismiss similar books, articles, and activists as part of some liberal conspiracy to upend biblical values or permit sexual promiscuity for its own sake. What animates these women is the fight against dehumanization and injustice—a deeply Christian impulse. Women are suffering all too frequently in our communities, and these authors want to see it stop. I do too. The more urgent ethical imperative of our time is not whether teenagers are having sex with their boyfriends and girlfriends. It is how we can stem the ongoing epidemic of abuse and dehumanization in our churches.

Allison is one person who has been harmed. The #ChurchToo hashtag she helped create documents the stories of hundreds. This movement has brought to light scandals that have shaken the foundations of some of the most prominent evangelical denominations in America, including the Anglican Church in North America and the Southern Baptist Convention.

If orthodoxy (right belief/worship) leads to orthopraxy (righteous living), then the harm and dehumanization running rampant in our churches should signal to us that all is not well with our theology. I care about theology, but in writing this book, I am animated by the sexual injustice I see in the church. Avoiding premarital sex is not a higher good than the fight against sexual violence, and yet I worry that we Christians too often act like it is. As Allison puts it, "Sometimes it feels like a whole generation of us were sacrificed on the altar of abstinence."[4]

COVERT MISOGYNY

Conservative Christian culture often preaches the importance of respect for women, but a not-so-subtle misogyny often lurks behind even the best intentions. Rachel Joy Welcher writes, "If women are expected to have a civilizing effect on men as purity culture teaches, then it is only reasonable to assume that when a husband acts uncivilized, his wife is at least partially responsible. . . . What might appear as respect for the female gender is actually an oppressive standard that assumes women can control the actions of men."[5] If we assume men cannot control their base impulses, it becomes difficult to hold them to a higher standard or pursue accountability for their sins against women. Welcher continues, "Purity teachings about the moral responsibility of women and the nature of male sexual lust position women as the guardians of sexual purity, so that when sexual purity is violated, it is women who are first and foremost on trial."[6]

Women aren't the only ones receiving these messages. Men are taught from a young age that they are, as men, particularly vulnerable to sexual sin. Because of this, it is incumbent on women and girls to not awaken men's sinful impulses. The subtext of these messages is that even the godliest men can't be expected to resist temptation if the visual, relational, or erotic stimulus is powerful enough. Again, the final responsibility is on women. Welcher writes, "The rhetoric of responsibility in some [purity culture] books instructs women to expect sexual harassment from men, leaving them with the weight of figuring out how to act, dress, and approach men in ways that discourage their lust."[7]

Like modern forms of racism, evangelical disdain for female bodies rarely takes the form of overt misogyny and prejudice (although it sometimes does). Usually it's much more subtle—so subtle that many men don't realize the ways they dehumanize and over-sexualize women.

THE OVERSEXUALIZATION OF WOMEN

Purity culture's toxic masculinity dehumanizes women by reducing their humanity and making it all about sex. If men are sex machines, women are machines for sex—objects of seduction toward sexual sin or the fulfillment of men's sexual urges. Christian oversexualization of women is a repressive oversexualization born out of a fear of female sexuality. If married or unmarried women "misbehave," men will fall and their spiritual lives will suffer. Women's sexual behavior is seen as the lynchpin for the integrity of the community; "*women's* sexuality must be just right, so that *men* can spiritually thrive."[8]

The regulation of women's clothing is central to this repression. Apparently, some men feel the only way to protect themselves from the dangers of female bodies is to literally keep women's bodies under wraps. Some men, it seems, can't bear the reminder that women are women—that they have breasts, hips, and midriffs. This puts Christian women in a precarious position. Julie, introduced in chapter two, put it this way: "I remember thinking that my body couldn't look any way but 'covered.' If a man saw my body and sinned, that would be my fault. I've deconstructed a lot of this, but to this day I get so stressed whenever I go shopping because of how deeply I internalized these ideas."

When I was in college, a regular topic of conversation was whether it was appropriate for Christian women to wear yoga pants in mixed company. Was this fashion choice considerate to the Christian men around them? Did it create too much of a stumbling block to the men in the community? These debates continued with some force for months, but eventually settled down. Some women wore the pants, others didn't. Most people just moved on.[9]

What's a man to do? Well, maybe nothing. Christian men shouldn't need to control others' clothing to avoid sexualizing them. Yes, clothing means something. Our clothes are not, as some suggest, merely a matter of personal expression with zero moral implications. All Christians, not just women, have a responsibility to think intentionally about the clothes they wear, but we must acknowledge that any attempt at standardizing appropriateness is subjective and culturally situated. Clothing styles and standards change; a man's responsibility remains the same.

Another common regulation is the so-called Billy Graham rule, popularized by Vice President Mike Pence, stating that a man, particularly a man in leadership, should never be alone with a woman other than his wife. Girls (and boys, for that matter) are given strict warnings about spending one-on-one time with someone of the opposite sex, to avoid communicating the wrong message or tempting the other to sexual sin.

Added together, these regulations communicate that women are a threat. As one woman put it, "[Women's] very femaleness felt like a weapon that [they] had no desire to wield."[10] Women don't need to do anything threatening to be viewed as hostile. The truth is that few women, and even fewer Christian women, intentionally use their sexuality to harm men. Despite this, Christian men often treat women like they are out to get them.

Some Christian men approach *all* interactions with women through a sexual lens. Is she dressed that way because she's trying to catch me in sin? Did she smile at me because she's flirting? If I'm single, is she attractive enough to warrant my attention? If I'm married, is she too attractive to warrant my attention? It's as if Christian men, single or married, are encouraged to size up every woman they meet in terms of whether she is trying to have sex with them. Don't flatter yourselves, guys.

Purity culture doesn't protect men—we can fall into sexual sin even with its regulations in place—it suppresses women. It hides women's female humanness from view: if men can't control themselves, women must exercise restraint and accommodate men's tendencies and instincts.

We should not be surprised when this posture of fear, antagonism, and dehumanization translates into abusive behavior. In Christian churches, overt hypersexualization of women is taboo, but subtle hypersexualization of women is not. You won't find catcalling, wet T-shirt contests, or boastful promiscuity in church. Since the subculture purports to honor women, the most egregious examples of dehumanization go into the shadows. Ironically, the stigma against sexual sin makes abuse harder to spot because no one would expect it of a "good Christian man." Tame dehumanization is the norm, but allegations of serious issues like child pornography, sexual abuse, coercion, and marital rape are often dismissed or ignored. Women are left to suffer in silence, even forced back into silence if they speak up, while men are allowed to wallow in ongoing sexual brokenness.

SEX, FOOD, AND "NEEDS"

Christian culture abounds with analogies and illustrations about sex—fire in fireplaces, petals of a flower, no-longer-sticky tape, the list goes on. An especially problematic one is the equating of sexual desire with the desire for food. The grain of truth in this analogy is that both the urge to eat and the urge to mate are experienced in and through the body. Likewise, both eating and procreating are linked to our survival instincts.

When we press this analogy too hard, however, it becomes easy to speak of the objects of our sexual desire as less than human. If the male desire for sex is like desire for a cheeseburger, a woman, even a wife, is a piece of meat. If this isn't dehumanization, I don't know what is. As with the regulations discussed above, we have reduced women's humanity to their sexuality, the potential of their bodies for an erotic encounter. Women are not sexual objects to be consumed. All Christian men would agree with this statement, but when we speak of our sexual "appetites," we imply as much. More importantly, it equates our access to food with access to sex. Food is crucial to our individual survival. Sex is not.

In late 2019, my wife's experience of childhood sexual abuse came to light. She began the long, difficult, and painful process of healing. Shelby and I sought the help of good therapists and psychologists, both for individual work and as a couple. In one of our couple's sessions, Shelby and I were describing the difficult state of our intimate relationship.

"It's really, really, really hard for me to think about having sex again," Shelby said through tears. "And I feel so awful because I know that's killing Zach, and I feel like I'm letting him down." She went on to describe how the more she processed and unpacked her history of abuse, the scarier the thought of resuming sexual activity became.

"Zach's a married man," Shelby continued. "He loves me, and I love him. As a man, this is something he should be able to have. Something I should be able to give him. It's something he needs. And I don't want him to leave me or be tempted to watch porn or anything like that." I was a mess of emotions during these sessions.

I was heartbroken to learn of my wife's sexual abuse. I wanted freedom for her. I wanted to support her as best I could. But the darker side of myself was frustrated that this meant I couldn't enjoy a sexual connection with my wife. I did feel like she was letting me down. I hated myself for feeling this way, but it was an undeniable part of my emotional experience at the time.

Our therapist nodded along with an empathetic expression. Then she said, "I hear you, Shelby. This is so hard because I can tell you love Zach so much. But remember that Zach doesn't need sex the way he needs food. A person can't survive without food, water, or sleep. But a person can survive without sex. We've been conditioned in the church as women to think that providing for our husbands sexually is like keeping them alive. But our bodies' relationships to food and sex are different."

Then the therapist turned and looked at me, "Zach, you can survive without sex."

I was stunned. On one level I knew this was true. But I had never thought of the way both Shelby and I had internalized my sexual needs as of equal importance to my need for food—as if asking me to go a few months or even a year without sex as a married man was tantamount to going a year without eating. I reflected on the way I had reduced Shelby to an outlet for my sexual appetite. I never realized I was dehumanizing her in this way. I had also sold myself short by believing I couldn't live as a faithful loving husband in a relationship where my sexual desires had been indefinitely put on the shelf.

SAVE THE WOMEN BY SAVING THE MEN

The healing of mine and Shelby's marriage was not simply a matter of her getting over her fear of sexual intimacy or processing her trauma. It was equally, if not more so, a matter of me unlearning my sense of sexual entitlement as a Christian man. This is what I mean when I say that addressing male dehumanization is key to rehumanizing women.

Our relationship serves as an illustration for the broader sexual dysfunction that plagues our communities. Paying due attention to the experiences of women, supporting them, and helping them heal from abuse and trauma—all of this is essential work of undoing the injustice caused by toxic masculinity. But this is only part of the work. To see real and lasting healing in our communities, men must unlearn toxic attitudes and behaviors and relearn what it means to live as whole and redeemed sexual beings.

The work of caring for the victims of abuse is essential, but until we speak to the men, we'll only be playing catch-up instead of addressing the problem itself. The root of abuse scandals in the church is a culture of toxic masculinity. It manifests in different ways and to different extents in various places. While it may not always qualify as abuse, the subtle dehumanization of women and men is all too prevalent.

I wasn't the one who abused my wife when she was a girl. That sin is not mine to bear. However, I realized during that counseling session (and the many that followed) that there was much I was responsible for in the sexual dysfunction of our relationship. I hadn't traumatized Shelby, but I had retraumatized her. Every time I felt entitled to her body, I dehumanized her. I never forced myself on her, but the toxic attitude of entitlement had formed my expectations for what sex in marriage should be. Until I changed, I was a hindrance to her healing.

REPENT AND BELIEVE THE GOSPEL

Mine is just one example of the way toxic masculinity manifests in Christian men and their relationships. If you're a man reading this, perhaps you have a sense of how your sexual brokenness has directly or indirectly, subtly or overtly, dehumanized women, children, other men, or yourself.

The first step toward healing wounds—both our own and the ones we have caused others—is repentance. I have no interest in making men feel bad about themselves for its own sake. Man hating does neither men nor women any good. Hating yourself or your sexuality is not the solution. However, if you want to find hope and healing, acknowledging the full extent of your brokenness and the harm you have caused is an important first step.

Dismantling toxic masculinity in our churches does not begin with writing books. For me and for you it begins with repentance. Admitting your brokenness—not to press deeper into shame and self-hatred but to free you to be who you were made to be.

Stop blaming women. Stop dehumanizing women. Stop dehumanizing yourself. Stop excusing your sin. Stop minimizing your sin. Stop hiding.

Believe that God loves and accepts you despite your brokenness. Believe that he can make you new. Believe that your broken masculinity is not beyond repair, that God wants to make you into something wonderful and beautiful—not despite your sexuality, but in and through it.

Partner with God in the work of rehumanization. Go to therapy. Talk to your pastor. Apologize to your wife.

Sexual brokenness can be the most difficult type of sin to own up to. The roots of shame run deep into our hearts and our souls. But the renewal of the world through the death and resurrection of Jesus involves every part of our humanity, including those sins we hesitate to acknowledge or would prefer to keep hidden. If you have partnered with the dehumanizing forces of darkness, God calls out to you in love, to partner in the work of making the world new again. He offers you not just forgiveness but a new way to live.

Repent and believe the gospel.

PART II

A RENEWED VISION OF MALE SEXUALITY

FIVE

VICTIMS OF OUR OWN DESIRE?

SHAME AND THE SHADOW OF MALE SEXUALITY

MY INTERVIEWEE CHRIS DESCRIBED his adolescent experience this way: "I remember feeling like the fact I was attracted to the female form was something bad about me. The message was that you're just as bad as a murderer or a child molester. You deserve hell because you find the female form attractive." Maybe you can relate. I know I can. In church we're taught to hate sin. We're told sin destroys us and separates us from God. We're told it makes us deserving of hell. Many teenage boys felt their sexuality was the main reason they committed sins. Chris went on, "If you hate your sexuality, you inevitably hate yourself. Because you can't separate yourself from your sexuality."

Hatred of our sexuality is hatred of our body because, as much as we may sometimes wish we could, we cannot separate our *self* from our body. An often-repeated criticism of purity culture is the way it led women and girls to hate and feel shame about their bodies, particularly the way their bodies supposedly threatened their communities by arousing sinful desire in the men around them.[1] But there is also a male side to body shame in purity culture. Where women and girls were shamed for the sexual thoughts they caused in others' bodies, men and boys often experienced shame for the sexual thoughts and feelings they *experienced* in their own bodies.[2]

Theologian Charles Marsh describes this experience powerfully in his memoir, *Evangelical Anxiety*: "[I had] a visceral sense . . . so often in my adolescence, of my body's disgrace, of my body as ground zero in a warfare between holiness, on the one hand, and the world, the flesh, and the devil on the other. The breakdown was an eruption of a body that was in a state of war with no promise of cease-fire on the horizon."[3]

Does hatred of the sexual self lead to healthy sexual behavior? Sadly, no. Most men and boys fail to live up to purity ideals. Sometimes purity culture addresses our failings, but the way it does often amounts to little more than a reinforcement of shame (even with an assurance of forgiveness) and new strategies for working harder to fight lust. This may seem like a sound approach on the surface, but the gospel isn't about working hard. In practice, the message of receiving forgiveness in Christ, plus strategies for fighting, is often insufficient for moving beyond unwanted sexual behavior. We're left feeling especially sinful or broken, like we aren't feeling bad enough, aren't working hard enough, or aren't believing the gospel in the right way.

Take pornography, for example. The stigma associated with porn use is strong in the church, which makes the cycle of shame associated with not being able to shake the habit that much stronger. The weight of guilt for many men can be crushing, especially when they feel alone in the struggle. "I felt like I was the only one dealing with this," Chris told me. "But as time went on and I talked to more of my friends about it I realized that it was an issue for just about everyone I knew. My friends sometimes looked at porn, and I didn't think they were so bad. Maybe I wasn't so bad either."

I don't think Chris was trying to excuse or minimize his porn use. He wasn't saying sin isn't real or that he should abandon his efforts to shake the habit. He was serious, as we all should be, about addressing dehumanizing patterns he saw in himself. He was merely realizing that this struggle didn't mean he was *especially* bad or broken, at least relative to his peers. Porn was a common problem, one that many young men were having a hard time navigating.

Men and boys often read the right books, join the right groups, memorize the right verses, set up the right software on their devices—all to no avail. Chris described an accountability group chat where he and his friends kept each other updated on their fight against lust. "I remember one time feeling like I needed to up the ante. I said, 'All right guys, if I look at porn, I'm literally going to pay you $50. We can donate it to a charity or something. I just need there to be consequences.'" Within a couple weeks, Chris had paid out $300 and realized maybe this wasn't the best idea.

A BROKEN VIEW OF OURSELVES

Guilt is the feeling I have done a bad thing or things. Shame is the feeling I am a bad or broken person.[4] Chris said he felt like his attraction to women was something bad about him. Teaching that a man's desire for sex is sinful reinforces a culture of shame around sexuality. It often leads to deeper entanglement in unwanted behaviors, further secrecy around sexual taboos, and an increased likelihood men will act out in destructive and dehumanizing ways. This could include obsessive pornography use, extramarital affairs, buying sex, and the abuse of women and children.

This broken vision isolates us as we start to believe we are undeserving of love, even of God's love. Psychologist and author Curt Thompson writes, "When we experience shame, we tend to turn away from others because the prospect of being seen or known by another carries the anticipation of shame being intensified or reactivated."[5] On one level, shame has a positive function. It can rightly signal to us that we have fallen short and drive us to make changes. But when we can't rise above the behavior causing our shame, we get stuck in a cycle of shame. This cycle drives us deeper and deeper into isolation, self-hatred, and secrecy. And secrets are the enemy of authentic human relationship. As Thompson writes, "We are only as sick as the secrets we keep. And shame is committed to keeping us sick."[6]

Too often, the only positive vision we cast for men about their sexuality is that it can be blessed by God if they manage to keep it in their pants until marriage. "Escape the shame by getting married"—not exactly a robust vision for the beauty of masculine sexuality. Men don't simply need new strategies for fighting the war against lust or a false assurance that it'll be okay once they get married. Men also need a renewed vision of what their sexuality is.

Often our effort-based strategies for fighting temptation are contrary to the spirit of the gospel. They're behavior modification, not transformation by the renewing of our minds. Jay Stringer writes,

> The gospel teaches us that we are beloved before any sexual sin or addiction entered into our lives, and we remain so, even at the height of our brokenness. When sin and addiction language overshadows this belovedness, the inevitable outcome is clinical and theological approaches that rely heavily on behavior modification. When sin and addiction language helps us reveal and connect us to our belovedness, the desire to change comes from our pursuit of beauty, not our self-contempt or latest strategy to combat sexual desire.[7]

Focusing on external behaviors isn't enough. Oftentimes, sexual sin is born out of deeper wounds and brokenness. It also flows from our view of ourselves. Until we correct the broken views of humanity that purity culture reinforces, we will find ourselves living into an old narrative that dehumanizes us and the people we love. Even if we do manage to get our behavior under control, the hypersexualized attitude toward ourselves and others will continue to inform how we view the world.

TOXIC NATURE, TOXIC HABITS

Male nature is sexual.[8] Men have capacities for sexual attitudes and behaviors. They have sexual organs, sexual urges, desires for relationship and connection, a capacity to give and receive pleasure, and a capacity to partner with a woman to create new life.

Having sexual capacities does not mean that all men act out their nature the same way. For example, all able-bodied people have the capacity to press keys on a piano since it's part of our nature to be able to move our fingers and thumbs. However, that isn't the same as being able to play a piano well. I took eight years of piano lessons as a kid, but when I try to play today, my ability is greatly diminished. My capacity to play hasn't changed, however. It is still part of my nature, even if I am no longer practiced in doing so.

My wife has done a much better job of keeping up the habit of playing piano. Shelby has a degree in music education, so her ability to play is more resilient than mine, and her skill stays higher, even if she hasn't practiced in weeks or months. (Shelby, for fear that some of you might mistake her for a concert pianist, has asked me to note that while she is more skilled than I, she is still a "mediocre pianist at best." I think she's being too modest.)

Now, a negative example. Able-bodied people can lift a foot and stomp it on the ground. My daughter Grace chooses to use this natural capacity to trample bugs. I don't know why, but she's done it enough that it's become a habit—a bad habit. No matter how many times we tell her it's cruel to kill bugs for no reason, she still feels the urge to crush them when she sees their tiny bodies crawling in front of her.[9]

How do we form habits? Lots of ways. We make choices that reinforce our future behavior patterns. Our environment, culture, and upbringing are also factors. Shelby worked hard to develop her musical habit, but she also had a home and church environment that supported her gift, along with resources to ensure she always had lessons and access to a decent piano for practice.

What if the habit of crushing bugs becomes so ingrained in Grace that she feels like she can't help but crush bugs whenever she sees them? What if a pianist becomes so adept at playing the instrument that even especially difficult pieces are effortless to play? When a habit, good or bad, develops to this point, we call it "second nature." It has become part of the person, and it's difficult for them to act otherwise.

Something similar has happened with toxic masculinity. Male nature is sexual, but toxic sexuality is not essential to masculine nature, nor is sexual brokenness the standard expression of male sinfulness. The dehumanizing and hypersexual impulses purity culture claims are part of being a man are not part of male nature. Instead, they are habits—more specifically, vices—men have been socialized into. True, the development of these habits is often a function of specific choices men made during their formative years. It is also a function of their environment, the teaching they received, their cultural context, and things that have been done to them or that they've been exposed to against their will.

Toxic masculinity is a formed habit, one that too many in our culture have learned. A habit that, for many of us, has become second nature. The good news is even our worst and most ingrained habits are still only *second* nature, which means they can be unlearned. If toxic masculinity has become second nature to many men, then a new type of masculinity can become second nature as well.

You don't fault a dog for barking. Dogs were made to bark. But you may scold a dog for barking nonstop, or for barking at a family member, or for refusing to stop barking when assured by its owner that all is well. Dogs bark, but their environment and training shape the way they bark. Likewise, we should not fault a man for being sexual. Men were made to be sexual. But men are responsible for the way they express their sexuality. If their sexual habits have developed in such a way that they harm and dehumanize themselves or others, they need to learn new habits.

JORDAN'S STORY

Jordan grew up in a Christian home. At a young age he lost his father to illness. Reflecting on this time in his life, he told me, "Suddenly there wasn't anyone looking over me or my brothers because my mom had to go to work. It seems like in that time anyone who could prey on a child came out of the woodworks." In a span of two years during elementary school, Jordan was "molested like crazy," including being raped by a member at his family's church. This particular abuser told Jordan, "This is something everybody does, but it's a secret. So don't tell anyone." These early experiences with sex and sexual violence primed Jordan for decades of shame and struggle. The church failed Jordan. It should have been a safe space for a vulnerable, grieving child. But things only got worse. The church was not just the setting for his trauma, it also became the context for repeated reenactments of the shame and brokenness Jordan felt about his sexuality.

Jordan's abuse didn't stay a secret for long. He began acting out in ways that raised red flags for his mother and stepdad. Jordan explained to me, "When you're abused as a kid, you don't know that the things that were done to you are wrong." Remember, Jordan was told by his abuser that this behavior was normal. So, he started doing the same things to other kids he knew.

When this came to light, Jordan's parents went to the pastor of their church who recommended a Christian therapist. In addition to a regular regimen of Scripture memory, this therapy involved traumatic psychological reenactments of Jordan's abuse.

> I had to sit down with people I had hurt or who had hurt me, then in detail, in front of an audience—I have no idea why anyone thought this was a good idea—describe every action that had occurred either to me or that I myself had done. That's when I first started experiencing shame around sex. No one told me, "You're a victim and these things shouldn't have

happened to you." It was just: "Pray this away. Confess all your sins, and then you're good." But that never really worked. No one really knew what to do with me. And no one ever really helped me work through or actually process what had happened to me.

In high school, when Jordan's mom and stepdad found out he was viewing pornography, he was placed in a Christian sex addiction recovery group alongside adult men who visited prostitutes and were serial adulterers. "It seemed really weird to me to be in a sex addiction group when I had never actually had consensual sex with a girl before." This group wasn't much more than a glorified Scripture-memory club. Despite Jordan's remorse about his on-going behavior and his desire to stop, the Scripture memory wasn't enough. This was, at best, an incomplete approach to the issues he was struggling with.

In the end, all the help Jordan received for his abuse and sexual behavior did little more than reinforce a deep sense of brokenness and shame. "I had been told my whole life sex was this awful thing and that I was no good for having that desire in my heart." Eventually, Jordan felt like he had nothing else to lose. "That became how I rebelled. And I leaned into it really, really hard. Not everybody who grows up in purity culture rebels in this way, but for me, I started sleeping with and hooking up with as many girls as I could. And I was proud of it, and I told everyone at my high school about it to prove I was fine."

Jordan couldn't suppress the shame because he couldn't suppress his sexual behavior. The church left him in a hopeless situation and reinforced his sense of brokenness. Jordan knew he had fallen short of the "stay pure" narrative he was provided. So, he leaned into a different narrative.

That's all I was: a sexual person. Every month or so, either in church or the Christian school I attended, I was told all these feelings in my body or all these thoughts in my head or all these things that I was doing are going to burn me up and lead me to eternal damnation. There's this struggle between this identity forced upon me and the fact that that identity made me completely unacceptable. It was a huge struggle. As I grew up, the conversation was never, "Your trauma lives on through your actions." It was always, "You are bad. And all these things are going to send you to hell and you need to stop." There was never any acknowledgment that human beings are supposed to be sexual.

Jordan grew distant from his upbringing and estranged from his faith. He struggled to cope in a dating relationship with a Christian girl who didn't want to have sex until marriage. At Jordan's insistence and coercion, they eventually did have sex. Racked by guilt, they decided to get married even though it was obvious their relationship was dysfunctional. Their union was unhappy, sexually stagnant, and it ended in devastation with mutual accusations of infidelity and loss of trust.

Today, Jordan is remarried, identifies as bisexual, and has left the church "for good." He continues to process a lot of his experiences, but he noted to me that his second wife is the first person who has made him feel accepted for being a sexual person—something he never experienced in Christian contexts.

ASKING BETTER QUESTIONS

What do we make of Jordan's story? It's undeniably tragic and full of pain. Would it be right to say that Jordan willfully disobeyed the commandments of the Bible or gave up on God's best for his sex life? I believe it's more complicated than that. The experience of shame, suffering, and retraumatization pushed him away from the church and toward dehumanizing behavior. Jordan himself admits he chose and is responsible for everything he did. Abusers are culpable for their behavior even when they have been abused themselves. Still, the teaching Jordan received failed to account for his own experience of abuse. The community around him failed to give him help and resources. Yes, Jordan is responsible, but it isn't entirely surprising that he acted out and rejected the moral standards he was taught. In that sense, I understand why Jordan left the church. It makes sense.

The dehumanizing treatment Jordan received, both from abusers and his church, perpetuated further dehumanizing behavior. The purity culture script he received—pray, memorize Bible verses, and your sexual brokenness will be healed—didn't lead to freedom. The intentions were good, and spiritual disciplines like prayer and Scripture meditation have been a staple of Christian faith and growth in godliness for centuries. But they are neither magical practices nor holiness pills. They should be integrated into a larger system of community formation, trauma-informed therapy, and the work of the Spirit.

Much of our approach to restoration from sexual brokenness amounts to what Larry Crabb calls "recipe theology,"[10] an approach to Christian living that imagines God has a straightforward, multi-step plan, or recipe, to address every issue or difficult circumstance we face in our lives. Do you struggle with sexual sin? Simply follow this proven five-step process and your life circumstances will improve! But life isn't this simple, as Jordan's story illustrates. Sometimes the path toward healing is complex, even mysterious. Sometimes restoration of our true, fully human selves involves a journey with no easy answers guaranteed to solve your problem in the coming days or weeks.

The people caring for Jordan should have focused on more than behavior modification for his pornography use. Like many aspects of purity culture, this approach doesn't account for the created goodness or the stunning complexity of human sexuality. Christians shouldn't watch porn, and they should think practically about how to avoid it and stop if they've developed a habit of doing so. However, compulsive pornography use is often a symptom of a deeper issue. Good doctors treat both symptoms and the underlying disease.

As Christians, we need to ask better questions of the sexual brokenness in ourselves and others. While we shouldn't under-spiritualize the dynamics at play, we should resist the urge to over-spiritualize them, especially if trauma and abuse are part of someone's story. Jay Stringer writes,

Healing requires you to pivot from condemning your lack of willpower to addressing the role trauma may be playing in your unwanted sexual behavior. A heart with an ounce of kindness for your life story will accomplish so much more for you than a mind filled to the brim with strategies to combat lust.[11]

Rules and strategies alone will not protect us, our children, or those in our ministries from sexual suffering, mistakes, and brokenness. Men and boys are responsible for their decisions, but the reasons they make those choices are much more complex than saying, "That's just how men are." There is no unified male sin nature. There is much more going on in each of us than a manifestation of a gendered sinful disposition.

Most of us don't need help feeling ashamed of our unwanted sexual behavior. Most Christian men indulging in sexual sin want to stop lusting after people at the gym, watching porn, or hooking up with people they have no intention of maintaining relationship with. They don't need to be yelled at and told they're horrible people. They already feel horrible, broken, and in many cases, unloved by God and undeserving of the love and affection of their family and friends.

Shame identifies men with their sexual brokenness. Their sins become who they are, not just things they do. Jordan felt like his sexuality was all that he was. If sexual brokenness was the totality of his identity, then the totality of his personhood was broken. Chris expressed it this way: "I felt like I was nothing more than a lustful teenager in the hands of an angry God." I remember having similar thoughts regarding my own struggles with pornography as a teenager. I felt like the fact that I looked at porn made me hopelessly broken and a sorry excuse for a Christian.

SHAME, CURIOSITY, AND THE FEAR OF SELF

From an early age many Christian boys are taught to fear their sexuality. The degree to which erotic curiosity is a natural, good, and even beautiful part of being a man is often not appreciated or understood. It makes sense that young people—boys and girls— are curious about sex. But churches and Christian homes aren't always safe spaces to explore this curiosity. The shame that young men feel for their sexuality is compounded, leading to a shame-fueled curiosity, absent of relationship, fixated on bodies rather than persons.

Stringer, again, writes:

> There is an unspoken rule in many homes and churches that sex is not to be talked about unless the conversation serves to put the fear of God in children about their participation in sex before marriage. Talking about sex solely in the context of prohibition, however, sets a child up for madness. A child needs to hear sex talked about in a way that honors the natural, God-given changes and desires that will accompany them from childhood to adulthood. An overemphasis on negative instruction about sex has the capacity to lead a child to associate sex with silence and shame. By the time the child reaches adulthood, this association becomes ingrained and continues to operate.[12]

This is why the shame-and-fear-fueled approach of purity culture serves to undermine its own goals. Boys are pressed further into isolation, and the silence, shame, and selfishness go with them into their adult lives, marriages, and church leadership positions.

Many of our parents and leaders were more concerned with ensuring we didn't do certain things rather than patiently guiding and being present with us no matter what we did. Control of behavior was more important than assurance of love and presence in our lives. Purity culture majors on preventing certain behaviors, but mistakes can't be fully avoided in a broken world. The desire of many parents to shield their children from suffering served instead to isolate them and push them away. This is what shame does. It isolates. It alienates. It breaks us apart from relationship with others, ourselves, and God.

THE GOODNESS OF SEXUALITY

Your pursuit of sex is a pursuit of something good. Your desire for sex is good. The desire isn't bad before marriage and good after marriage. The sexual nature that makes you desire sex, whether you're married or not, is good. This doesn't mean every sexual impulse should be acted on. These impulses are often born out of habits, good or bad, that qualify our sexual nature. But our desire for human connection, love, and acceptance from women and men is good. God loves us in our brokenness, but having a sexual nature doesn't make us broken. At worst, our sexual inclinations are a misdirection of something good.

Shame can be a healthy and appropriate response to the realization that we have dehumanized ourselves and others. But for some of us, the guilt we feel about our sexual brokenness has morphed into a cycle of shame that drives us further into dehumanization and away from relationship with God and others. It makes us believe that our sexual bodies and the desires they stir in us are, in and of themselves, things to be ashamed of. But this is not a message from God. It is a message from Satan.

Everything God made is good; he said so after every act of creation. Your sexuality is better than neutral—it's good. But even in its innate goodness, our sexuality can be directed toward humanizing or dehumanizing ends. We need direction, help, education, and renewal to grow into what our sexuality was meant to be. It shouldn't sit idle and under wraps. God isn't embarrassed by it, and we shouldn't be either.

SIX

THE BIBLE SAYS SO

CORRECTING MISCONCEPTIONS ABOUT THE BIBLE AND MALE SEXUALITY

DURING MY SOPHOMORE YEAR IN COLLEGE, I attended a conference hosted by my home church, which included conversations between well-known megachurch pastors. In one of the sessions, my senior pastor asked one of the guest speakers, "Does viewing pornography disqualify someone from serving in ministry?"

The guest responded without hesitation, "No question. Particularly if it's regular and habitual."

The host then asked, "What kind of frequency are we talking here? Once a week, once a month, once a quarter, once a year?"

This time the guest pastor hesitated slightly. "I mean, once a week, once a month, once a quarter—because that's habitual. That's a problem."

My body tensed and my face flushed. I was grateful for the low lighting in the room, and I did my best to seem unbothered by his response. It didn't surprise me, but hearing it said out loud was difficult. This easily disqualified me from being a pastor. I also suspected it disqualified many, if not most, of the young men in the room.

I steeled myself again for renewed fervor in my fight against lust and sexual sin. I went back to my dorm that day and reread a purity culture classic on resisting sexual temptation and lust. I hated my sexuality, and I had decided again, for the hundredth time, to kill my sin, to put to death what was earthly in me.

I nodded along with familiar shame-fueled seriousness as I read. At one chapter's conclusion, the author argued Scripture memorization was key in our fight against lust, quoting Psalm 119:11, "I have hidden your word in my heart, that I might not sin against you." He went on to list no less than twenty additional Scripture passages that could be used to combat the devil and the flesh in moments of temptation. He concluded with a challenge, to memorize every verse he listed.

Challenge accepted, I thought.

I did it. I wrote each one on an index card, carried them with me everywhere, and had each one memorized within a week and a half. Surely, this would be the silver bullet in my fight against porn and masturbation. God's Word is powerful, after all. The devil and his temptations didn't stand a chance.

The memorized Scripture worked pretty well.

Until it didn't. About two weeks later.

THE BIBLE AND PURITY CULTURE

Why do I tell this story? I don't mean to imply that Scripture memorization is useless—far from it—but even the sincerest application of Scripture memory is not the silver bullet it's often made out to be. If the Bible isn't a magical cure-all in our fight against temptation, how does it relate to our discussion of male sexuality?

Virtually everyone who grew up in purity culture also grew up around a high (and literalistic) view of the Bible. The ideals of purity culture were placed alongside respect for biblical authority, whether or not Scripture explicitly taught them. For instance, some people came to view saving your first kiss for the wedding day as a matter of Christian and biblical faithfulness, even though no such admonition appears in Scripture.

For many, deconstructing their view of the Bible goes hand in hand with deconstructing purity culture, primarily because views on purity, abstinence, and dating were framed as the clear teaching of the Bible. For some of you, Scripture feels restrictive, coercive, to this day. It was used to shame you or control you. When you had questions, verses were used to shut you up.

I understand many who are reading this book may be reevaluating their relationship with the Bible. While I still affirm the final authority of Scripture for the Christian life, my view has shifted from when I was younger. I want to be respectful of where people see themselves, and I don't want to use the Bible to strong-arm anyone into a certain view of human sexuality (even if that view is a revision of purity culture norms). Still, I feel it's important to talk about Scripture because of the close relationship between purity culture and the Bible in many people's lives.

When we come to the Bible with preconceived notions about the world or ourselves, we will see only what we expect to see instead of hearing from God or the ancient authors. For instance, conservatives with a predisposition toward patriarchal gender roles will see support for their view. Other Christians will place greater emphasis on the Bible's messages of liberation and female empowerment. Our blindness, brokenness, and bias filter what we're willing to see in Scripture. As Jonathan Grant writes, "It seems that Scripture cannot be allowed to contradict our deepest impulses."[1] This is a problem for both progressives and conservatives. Any of us, no matter our ideological persuasion, can fall into the trap of reading the Bible only to reinforce our assumptions when, at times, it should be challenging them.

Purity culture often reads into the Bible a particular vision of masculine sexuality, rather than reading out of it and letting Scripture challenge our assumptions about patriarchy and manhood. As it turns out, the New Testament authors weren't all that interested in helping men become more manly, find a smoking hot wife, and have mind-blowing sex on God's terms. This may seem obvious, but it's worth saying because many of us were raised to believe that the Bible was primarily about this sort of thing. Rather, the Bible's primary concern is with the redemption of this broken world through the death and resurrection of Jesus of Nazareth, the promised Jewish Messiah.

Still, the Bible does have some things to say about sexuality and masculinity, and for the remainder of this chapter, we'll look at a few of the "biblical" assumptions many of us heard growing up.

ARE MEN MORE SEXUAL THAN WOMEN?

"Men are only interested in one thing, and that's sex." This is a well-worn trope of films and entertainment. The sex-obsessed, emotionally stunted womanizer is a standard character in many sitcoms. See Joey Tribbiani in *Friends* or Barney Stinson in *How I Met Your Mother*.

Some Christians have adopted an extreme version of this cultural assumption.[2] It's as if we've assumed that erotic obsession is the destiny of every man, and that this is an essential difference between men and women. The scientific evidence is more complicated than it's made out to be,[3] and Christians who claim to derive their understanding of human nature from Scripture should stop to ask if the Bible teaches such a simplistic view of men.

Christians are often socialized to expect that a husband's sexual desire will far outweigh that of his wife. A book that was formative for me in high school claimed that men tend to be more interested in the physical and sexual aspects of marriage while women tend to value the love and companionship aspects. Christian teaching and preaching often reflect these sentiments, even if it's not stated explicitly. So, if a wife never wants to have sex with her husband, it is considered normal. Perhaps the disinterest many Christian women have toward sex is because their natural desire for sexual intimacy has been stolen from them. Maybe it's because they've been told their desire should be less intense than the men around them. Like the hypersexualized view of men we've already discussed, I fear this undersexualized view of women becomes a self-fulfilling prophecy. Women can't win in purity culture. On the one hand their bodies are oversexualized, as we've discussed, and on the other hand, they're told that having erotic thoughts is unladylike.

While men often report higher levels of libido, erotic desire is not uniquely male. I challenge you to produce a passage of Scripture that teaches men are more sexual or erotic than women. Someone may point to the warnings of Proverbs 5, in which a father speaks to his son about avoiding adultery with another man's wife. This text, like many in the Bible, is written by a man to men. The message could easily be transposed into a female key, with a mother warning her daughter against committing adultery with another woman's husband.

Let's not forget that it is the woman who speaks most in the Song of Songs, including some of the most erotic passages. For example:

I slept but my heart was awake.
    Listen! My beloved is knocking:
"Open to me, my sister, my darling,
    my dove, my flawless one.
My head is drenched with dew,
    my hair with dampness of the night."
I have taken off my robe—
    must I put it on again?
I have washed my feet—
    must I soil them again?
My beloved thrust his hand through the latch-opening;
    my heart began to pound for him.
I arose to open for my beloved,
    and my hands dripped with myrrh,
my fingers with flowing myrrh,
    on the handles of the bolt. (Song 5:2-5)

If you're wondering if this passage means what you think it means—it does. And I get it if finding a description like this in the Bible surprises you or makes you uncomfortable. However, I don't think we should be shy about what the biblical author is describing: intense *female* sexual desire. It is beyond me that a religious tradition with Scripture containing such a text came to believe eroticism was a male characteristic.

To desire sex isn't male. It is human. There's nothing inherently feminine about having little or no sexual desire. Women experience all ranges of sexual temperaments, and there's nothing unfeminine or inappropriate about this.[4] Similarly, one man may have acute experiences of sexual longing, while another man may not. Neither one is more nor less a man because of this. We may observe certain patterns in society, but these patterns are themselves a function of complex social pressures, media portrayals, and historical narratives—not raw biology. Prescribing these stereotypes as a test of "real" masculinity or femininity is not a Christian or biblical way to think about desire.

IS *PURITY* A SEXUAL TERM?

Psalm 119:9 reads, "How can a young man keep his way pure? By guarding it according to your [God's] word" (ESV). Given our assumptions about masculinity, many Christians read, "How can a young man avoid sexual sin? By memorizing Bible verses." But this is not what the verse says, and there are two problems with this interpretation. The first problem is with the word translated "young man." I grew up reading the 1984 version of the NIV, which reads "How can a *young man* keep his way pure?" (emphasis mine). The ESV maintains the literalistic translation "young man" for the Hebrew *naar*, which means "youth" or "lad," and it often is used to refer specifically to a male youth (e.g., Gen 21:12). But the word also has a feminine form, *naarah*, which appears, for example, as "young women" in Ruth 2:22. The 2011 NIV translates Psalm 119:9, rightly in my view, as "How can a *young person* stay on the path of purity?" (emphasis mine). The context in the psalm does not suggest a narrow reference to young boys, but rather an inclusive use of the masculine noun to refer to young people in general.[5] The second problem with this popular interpretation of Psalm 119:9 has to do with the Hebrew word *zakah* ("to be/make pure"). This term has no direct connotation of virginity or sexual chastity. It simply means to be unstained. Metaphorically, it is often applied to being morally clean, but even this is not necessarily sexual. When we sexualize this term, I suspect it says more about our own shame than what the Bible teaches us about sexual behavior.

While I was growing up, seeing the word *purity* in the Bible always triggered sexual associations. This included some of the best-known verses in Scripture, like when Jesus said, "Blessed are the pure in heart, for they will see God" (Mt 5:8); or the psalmist, "Who may ascend the mountain of the LORD? Who may stand in his holy place? The one who has clean hands and a pure heart, who does not trust in an idol or swear by a false god" (Ps 24:3-4). There's nothing explicitly sexual to be found in these verses, much less any references to remaining pure for a future spouse. The biblical call to purity isn't merely a call to avoid sexual sin. It's so much more.

In the Old Testament, the prophet Isaiah rebukes the ancient Israelites by telling them to cleanse and purify themselves. Someone who grew up in purity culture might suspect such a statement is directed at their sexual sin. But look at what Isaiah says: "Wash and make yourselves clean [pure]. Take your evil deeds out of my sight; stop doing wrong. Learn to do right; seek justice. Defend the oppressed. Take up the cause of the fatherless; plead the case of the widow" (Is 1:16-17). Isaiah says nothing about sexual sin. He points to larger patterns of injustice and oppression. These are the sins God is calling them to repent of. If we want to pursue biblical purity, we would do well to broaden our categories.

Does the Christian call to purity include sexuality? Absolutely. However, narrowing purity to sexual categories causes us to misunderstand biblical language. Therefore, I have avoided language of "sexual purity" in this book, except when critiquing purity culture. Purity language has too many associations, and many of them aren't all that biblical. Moreover, we as a church too often neglect what biblical authors like Isaiah *did* have in mind when they exhorted God's people toward purity. When we embody a more holistic vision of biblical purity, perhaps we'll be able to speak about how that vision affects our sexuality. For now, we would do well to repent of the hypocrisy revealed by our overemphasis on certain types of sexual impurities at the expense of what Jesus calls "the more important matters of the law—justice, mercy, and faithfulness" (Mt 23:23).

We misread other terms and passages too. Another classic example is Proverbs 4:23, which reads, "Above all else, guard your heart, for everything you do flows from it." This verse is also not about keeping a pure heart for your future spouse, but how many of us were told that "guarding our hearts" was all about dating relationships? The Hebrew term for heart (*leb*) does not have the romantic connotations of its English counterpart. That said, is it wrong to caution teenagers about getting too emotionally invested in juvenile romances? Not at all. Is this the point of this verse? Also no. The problem isn't with the advice; it's with the narrow and shallow view of the Bible.

Another example is the exhortation girls and women receive about not "causing their brother to stumble" by wearing tight or revealing clothing, language taken from Romans 14:20 and 1 Corinthians 8:13. Both passages in their context focus on being considerate of other Christians whose personal convictions about food offered to idols differ from one's own. Neither passage has anything to do with inadvertently eliciting lustful thoughts from men because of the clothing one wears.

When we sexualize and romanticize terminology in the Bible, I suspect it often has more to do with us and our cultural context than what the Bible itself says. The sexual lens for interpreting biblical exhortations often leaves out much of the Bible's historical and theological significance. And sometimes, we're just making the Bible say what we think it should say.

IS SEXUAL FRUSTRATION A GOOD REASON TO GET MARRIED?

First Corinthians 7 contains the longest sustained teaching on sex and marriage in the apostle Paul's letters. He begins, "Now for the matters you wrote about: 'It is good for a man not to have sexual relations with a woman.' But since sexual immorality is occurring, each man should have sexual relations with his own wife, and each woman with her own husband" (vv. 1-2). A few verses later, he writes, "Now to the unmarried and the widows I say: It is good for them to stay unmarried, as I do. But if they cannot control themselves, they should marry, for it is better to marry than to burn with passion." (vv. 8-9). Is marriage God's provision for our sexual frustrations? In one sense, yes. Men and women with sexually healthy marriages may experience some relief from temptation and sexual frustration. But does this mean that the married are free from temptation to sexual sin? Absolutely not.

Paul is responding to a group of Corinthian Christians who believed being single was a godlier state than marriage. He does admit single people have greater freedom to serve God—a theme picked up by many Christian traditions throughout history—but he rejects the notion that being married is itself bad or inferior. Some Corinthians were avoiding marriage while giving into sexual urges in other ways (likely with temple prostitutes). Paul rightly points out their hypocrisy. There's no reason to avoid getting married if you want to be married. This is what Paul means when he says it is better to be married than to avoid it while indulging in sexual sin.

He does not, however, offer marriage as a cure-all to our sexual frustration, as common as this view is in churches today. If you're single, marriage will not solve your sexual problems. If you go into marriage thinking it will soothe the emptiness in your soul that leads you to harmful sexual behavior, you're setting yourself up for marital struggle. Young men and women should not view each other as a cure-all for their sexual needs. If you're with someone you love and care about—and you're able to responsibly start a life together—then get married. Don't do it just because you want to have sex. If you enter marriage viewing your wife as the release valve for pent-up sexual frustration, you're starting that relationship on a dehumanizing and misogynistic note.

DO WIVES OWE HUSBANDS SEX?

Before leaving 1 Corinthians 7 (for now), we should discuss another common facet of contemporary Christian teaching. Beginning in verse 3, Paul writes:

> The husband should fulfill his marital duty to his wife, and likewise the wife to her husband. The wife does not have authority over her own body but yields it to her husband. In the same way, the husband does not have authority over his own body but yields it to his wife. Do not deprive each other except perhaps by mutual consent and for a time, so that you may devote yourselves to prayer. Then come together again so that Satan will not tempt you because of your lack of self-control. (vv. 3-5)

Is a wife in sin if she declines sex with her husband? Look at what Paul says. This passage is not about the obligations of wives to their husbands, but about the obligations of both husbands and wives to each other. In Paul's world, the idea that a husband's body belonged to his wife was radical and countercultural. This passage empowered women to expect—even demand—their husband's sexual faithfulness. A further application is that there should be a mutuality of service in the marital sexual relationship. Some Christian men have used 1 Corinthians 7 to spiritually abuse their wives and coerce them into obligatory sex. I wonder if the same men would see themselves as violating Paul's teaching in their unwillingness to sexually service their wives after demanding service from her.

There are times and seasons in a marriage when you need to abstain from sexual activity. Women understand this because it's written into their bodies. The cycles of menstruation, pregnancy, childbirth, and breastfeeding take an enormous toll. Beyond embodied realities unique to women, we could add chronic illness, depression, disability, and more. Its unkind and unloving for men to expect sexual activity during times of immense physical or emotional strain, and women shouldn't feel pressured to give it. If a woman chooses to engage sexually, well and good. She should not feel like her husband's sexual integrity is at stake if she doesn't.

Sometimes it is sinful to demand marital rights. Sexual connection can (and should!) be a way spouses serve and care for each other. But a spouse is not a crutch for a lack of self-control. Paul is exhorting men and women not to weaponize sex in their relationship. Don't hold it over each other or use it as a tool to deprive your partner. Even though regular sexual connection may protect us from some measure of temptation, it does not excuse us from our responsibility of growing in self-control. We'll have more to say about sexual dynamics in marriage in chapter thirteen.

TWO BIBLICAL MEN

The story of David's adultery with Bathsheba (2 Sam 11) is often held up as a cautionary tale in purity culture. David, the greatest king in the history of Israel, the man after God's own heart, was vulnerable to sexual sin. Indeed, this is a cautionary tale, but not a caution against loose women who try to seduce godly men. Bathsheba is not the instigator here. This story looks a lot like what we would describe today as sexual coercion: that is, rape. As king, David is in a position to demand sex from any woman he wishes, and he uses that power to proposition another man's wife. With her husband away, Bathsheba is vulnerable to David's toxic advances.

Christian men beware, lest you become like David. Don't use your power, strength, position, or privilege to sexually harm and take advantage of the vulnerable. David is the assailant. Bathsheba is the victim, not the seductress.

On the other hand, Genesis 39 tells the story of Potiphar's wife's attempt to seduce Joseph. Here the woman is the one with the power. Joseph is a servant; she is the mistress of the house. Joseph resists her advance, and she reframes the encounter to make Joseph out to be the assailant. Joseph's integrity costs him dearly, and he loses his honored position and is put in prison. The moral here is not simply that men should watch out for women like Potiphar's wife. Nor is the point of the passage that we should be paranoid that a woman will attack us with a false accusation. God blesses and provides for Joseph in prison, eventually providing an opportunity to serve in the house of Pharaoh. This again proves the overall point of the Joseph narrative—that even what people mean for evil God can turn for good (Gen 50:20). Genesis 39 is not a cautionary tale about avoiding false accusations; it's a reassuring story, showing that even if you are falsely accused, God will take care of you. Joseph is a godly example of how to resist sexual temptation. He understands that sleeping with another man's wife would not just be a sin against Potiphar but ultimately a sin against God (Gen 39:9).

These two stories are not trying to teach us something about the women involved. They're showing us two different types of men. David was a man who lacked integrity and self-control in his sexuality. Joseph was a man who knew that he could resist sexual temptation.

Guys, don't be like David. Be like Joseph.

Yes, the stories in Scripture serve as examples for us, but the Bible is much more than a collection of cautionary tales. It includes advice, even laws about sexual behavior, but it's far more than a rule book for sexual ethics. Scripture memorization can be a useful tool in fighting temptation, but the Bible is not a magical book of spells that we can memorize for guaranteed results in our struggle against sin.

There's another man in the Bible we haven't talked about yet. What does Jesus have to do with our sexuality? What does he have to do with being a man? What does the story of redemption told in Scripture have to do with toxic masculinity?

SEVEN

THE TRUE MAN

JESUS AND THE REDEMPTION OF THE MALE BODY

"IT'S A WONDERFUL THING TO BE A MAN."

My therapist kept talking as I sat dumbstruck. In that moment, and in many other moments throughout my life, being male felt anything but wonderful.

This was a one-on-one session, separate from our couple's therapy, and with a different therapist. It had consisted of a conflict between two parts of myself. The first part wanted nothing more than to love and support my wife by giving her needed space to heal from her trauma revelations. The other part of me wanted to have sex, feel accepted, loved, and served by her in my own feelings of loneliness and rejection. I tried desperately to keep my sexual desires under control. I felt horrible, dirty, and selfish. Shelby's world had been turned upside down and she was reeling with trauma flashbacks and triggers. Still, sometimes all I could think about was the fact that I hadn't had sex in weeks.

I was disgusted with myself in these moments. Maybe you're disgusted with me as you read this. I get it. Or maybe it reminds you of your own attitude toward sex in one way or another. My inability to suppress my desires brought back a heavy weight of shame from my younger years. During this therapist-recommended season of abstinence, I was sometimes tempted to watch porn.

I hadn't done so in a few years, and I had developed enough maturity and emotional awareness to know this would only make me feel worse.

What about masturbating without watching porn? I had a couple decades' worth of shame-filled associations with masturbation—the secrecy, the sense of moral and spiritual failure. I couldn't shake the vague sense it was wrong for me to masturbate at all. My Christian therapists assured me masturbation was perfectly okay given my circumstances. Theologically, I wasn't so sure. To make matters more complicated, years of purity culture messaging stuck with me and my body. Old emotional habits die hard.

My feelings weren't rooted only in residual shame either. It felt violating of Shelby to fantasize about having sex with her when the real her—her embodied, present self—had no interest in being intimate. Even the thought of sex was scary for her. Was I supposed to mentally pretend she did want to have sex with me? To gratify and give myself release felt like a form of mental assault—if there is such a thing. It felt dehumanizing. It felt like lust.

I had spent the session telling my therapist I couldn't masturbate without feeling horrible and described how my wife's reactions to my body made me feel lonely and rejected. I explained how my fantasies, arousal, and desire for Shelby filled me with shame. My body felt disgusting. The sexual parts of me were emblematic of all that was selfish and shameful about me. Who would deliver me from this body of death?

My therapist paused for a few weighty seconds after I finished my I-wish-I-could-turn-off-my-sexuality rant. Then he said, "Zach, I want you to close your eyes and breathe deeply in and out." More silence. Then, "Zach, I want you to think about your body. Your maleness. If you can, I want you to think about your body in a state of arousal. Not having sex or doing anything sexual, not even necessarily with another person there. Just you. Alone with your body.

Think about the fact that God made you and your body. That it's beautiful and delightful to him."

That's when he said it. "It's a wonderful thing to be a man."

A lump formed in my throat. Tears welled in my eyes.

My therapist continued. "The male body in a state of arousal is a wonderful thing. There's so much vitality. There's a type of anticipation, expectation. There's a hope for a transcendent experience of relationship, of pleasure, of life. There's the potential for new life, as well as the potential for a beautiful type of risk, vulnerability, and adventure. When your body experiences sexual desire, it's doing exactly what it was made to do. That's a good thing. And it's nothing to be ashamed of. It's wonderful and beautiful. It's a gift to you and to the world."

RESURRECTING MALE SEXUALITY

Some men live in unacknowledged fear of their bodies. We feel like our sexuality is only bad, our desires are only dark, that this part of ourselves is irredeemable. But this isn't true. The Christian gospel announces that our bodies can be redeemed in Christ. Why is the superficial, legalistic approach of purity culture often so ineffective in curbing toxic masculinity in Christian men? Because it deals in a truncated, false gospel. Rules and regulations for sexual behavior don't make men new. Rather, the renewal of our minds and bodies by the Holy Spirit is the solution to the broken masculinity that plagues our culture and churches.

The Christian vision for sexuality isn't a moral add-on to the story of redemption. It's inseparable from it. Christian sexual ethics have no meaning apart from incarnation, death, and resurrection. Renewed masculinity is not a matter of mental assent to a set of doctrines or a commitment to male leadership in the home and in society. It's not even about adherence to a specific expression of Christian sexual ethics. Renewed masculinity is a matter of death and resurrection.

Toxic masculinity comes to be when embodied male advantage combines with the dehumanizing force of sin. Sin isn't just the bad things we do. It is the breaking of our humanity, falling short of who we were created to be. Toxic masculinity manifests in the things we do, yes, but it is caused by a deeper fracture. Many of us, Christian or not, understand our need for forgiveness, but we also understand we need more than forgiveness. We need more than rules. We need to be healed.

The story of the Bible is about more than forgiveness and going to heaven when you die. It's the story of how God entered creation to renew and heal it. This story has everything to do with the goodness, brokenness, and redemption of our sexual bodies.

JESUS, THE TRUE MAN

The Christian doctrine of the incarnation teaches that the eternal Son of God took on flesh and became human as Jesus of Nazareth—God in *carne*, the Latin word for "flesh" or "meat." The world into which Christianity emerged did not have a high view of human bodies. Platonic dualism associated with Greek philosophy viewed fleshly, bodily existence as lower and less dignified than non-bodily spiritual things. Bodies, they taught, were polluted by decay and carnal desires, like the desire for sex.

It was difficult for some Greeks and Romans to accept the Christian message. Many doubted that a dignified and spiritual being like a god, much less the Creator God Jews claimed to worship, could become human. At best, a god could pretend to be human, putting on the illusion of a human body. And this is exactly what some early members of the Jesus movement said: that Jesus wasn't actually human. He was the Son of God appearing to be a human since it would be impossible for a god to take on flesh. This view of Jesus came to be known as Docetism,[1] a heretical belief that the Son of God appeared to be human but did not take on a human nature.

The apostles and church fathers countered this and similar claims from the earliest days of Christian history, saying Jesus was a true human being. John writes in 1 John 4:

> Dear friends, do not believe every spirit, but test the spirits to see whether they are from God, because many false prophets have gone out into the world. This is how you can recognize the Spirit of God: Every spirit that acknowledges that Jesus Christ has come in the flesh is from God, but every spirit that does not acknowledge Jesus is not from God. (vv. 1-3)

For the apostle John, an important mark of Christian faithfulness is whether someone confessed the true humanity of Jesus.

The author of Hebrews tells us Jesus was like us in every way, "yet he did not sin" (Heb 4:15). This means he had a fully human body, just like the one you and I have. He was subject to all our limitations, our emotional experiences of sorrow, loneliness, and anger. He was subject to our physicality, including all the less-than-polished aspects we're tempted to be ashamed of—sickness, bodily fluids and waste, our need for food, sleep, physical contact, and relationship.

We have more in common with the ancient Greeks than we realize. We, too, hate our bodies. We want to escape from their limitations and contingencies, their subjection to death. The incarnation is more than a technical point of theology. It shows how God feels about the human body. Humanity was not too broken, disgusting, or irredeemable that God couldn't bear to inhabit a human body. That God created human bodies and declared them good was already a stunning affirmation of the glory and dignity of embodiment. Then God went even further. In the incarnation, God *inhabits* our broken humanity. Even in our sin, God has not rejected our bodies. As we often reject and move away from our embodiment, God, in Christ, moves toward us.

"JESUS HAS A PENIS"

If you grew up in the church, there's a good chance you've heard a lot of this before, but we often fail to go the extra step and consider what Jesus' humanity means for our sexuality. Sermons focused on Jesus' humanity may discuss his human need for rest and food. Or, if the preacher is feeling edgy, they may talk about Jesus' need to use the bathroom—whatever that looked like in first-century Palestine.

One Sunday in my midtwenties, I heard a different type of sermon.[2] The pastor at our church was discussing this exact point, the humanity of Jesus. Then he pivoted to the sexuality of Jesus. To be human is to be sexual, he argued, and Jesus had a male sexual body.[3] This includes parts common to all humans—eyes, ears, nipples, fingers, toes—and those distinct to male embodiment—facial hair, broader shoulders relative to women, and a penis.

"Jesus had a penis. Think about that fact for a moment," the pastor said. This wasn't a perverted or immature comment. It was a profound, theological point. When discussing Jesus' humanity, we often skip over his sexuality, effectively neutering him or making him androgenous. But that's not true humanity. True humanity is sexual or sexed. All human bodies are sexed, and even the minority of people born with bodies that do not conform to our common categories—male and female—are born with sexual bodies.

That Jesus has a penis is a healing message for men who struggle to love and accept their sexual selves. Sometimes the reason we're comfortable with Jesus being fully human is because we've mentally neutered his humanity. As soon as we start thinking about Jesus having a penis, the incarnation makes us uncomfortable. We don't want Jesus tangled up with all the mess and complexity of our sexual bodies, but the reality is, as Charles Marsh writes, "The Word made flesh is messy business."[4]

There is no asexual human body.[5] When we hide from or refuse to acknowledge that Jesus had a sexed body, we deny the truth of the incarnation. If we think it's shameful to think about Jesus having a penis, perhaps, more than anything, that shows the shame we feel about our own individual or collective sexuality as humans. By neutering Jesus, are we denying that Christ has come in the flesh? Are we espousing the ancient heresy of Docetism? In our hearts do we think that Jesus only appeared to be male? Do our minds recoil at the thought of his sexed body? Remember, any spirit that denies that Christ has come in the flesh is not from God.

JESUS AND THE NEW HUMANITY

What did Jesus' expression of masculine sexuality look like? For starters, he was single and never had sex.[6] Would any Christian suggest that these qualities kept Jesus from being a real man? Of course not. If anything, Jesus' life radically dignifies singleness. It shows that being a good Christian man and living out faithful male sexuality isn't about having a wife and kids. We don't know the details of Jesus' experience of sexual desire, but because it is part of being human, we should acknowledge the likelihood that he did experience it (Heb 4:15). Desire itself is not sinful.[7] We don't need to make Jesus asexual to maintain that he is holy and sinless.

Jesus was also a staunch defender of women who were shamed by the culture (Lk 7:36-50; 8:1-3; Jn 4; 8). He *rehumanized* these women, showing us what humanity was supposed to be all along. He is more human than any person who ever lived because he never treated himself or anyone else in a dehumanizing way. He was the new and better Adam. Here's how Paul described it in Romans 5:

> Therefore, just as sin entered the world through one man, and death through sin, and in this way death came to all people, because all sinned. . . . For if the many died by the trespass of the one man, how much more did God's grace and the gift that came by the grace of the one man, Jesus Christ, overflow to the many! . . . For just as through the disobedience of the one man the many were made sinners, so also through the

obedience of the one man the many will be made righteous. (vv. 12, 15, 19)

Jesus obeyed where Adam disobeyed, and just as sin and brokenness entered the world through Adam, life and justice can re-enter the world through Jesus. His expression of masculine sexuality looks radically different compared to our contemporary cultural expressions, both inside and outside of the church. As a male, he participated in what I have described as male embodied advantage, but he never indulged in the dehumanizing aspects of male sexuality that have plagued human societies. Jesus did not participate in sexual conquest, sexual entitlement, lustful fantasy, or a fear of women. He affirmed the goodness of both singleness and marriage (Mt 19:1-12) and never suggested that the only way to avoid sexual sin is to be married. Jesus is more than a good example of restrained, rehumanizing masculine sexuality. In his death, Jesus took on himself not just the punishment for our sexual sins, but the brokenness of our bodies. This includes our fractured and dehumanized masculinity.

Finally, Jesus' resurrection inaugurates a new, renewed humanity. Paul writes to the Corinthians about Jesus' resurrection:

> But Christ has indeed been raised from the dead, the first-fruits of those who have fallen asleep. For since death came through a man, the resurrection of the dead comes also through a man. For as in Adam all die, so in Christ all will be made alive. . . . The first man was of the dust of the earth; the second man is of heaven. As was the earthly man, so are those who are of the earth; and as is the heavenly man, so also are those who are of heaven. And just as we have borne the image of the earthly man, so shall we bear the image of the heavenly man. (1 Cor 15:20-22, 47-49)

Jesus takes us off the path of dehumanization that ends in hell and the destruction of our humanity. By the Spirit of God, he places us back on the path of rehumanization, making us into the humans we were always meant to be. We can live in anticipation of our future, renewed humanity, even as we await our coming resurrection and wholeness. Paul writes in Romans 8:

> We ourselves, who have the firstfruits of the Spirit, groan inwardly as we wait eagerly for our adoption to sonship, the redemption of our bodies. For in this hope we were saved. But hope that is seen is no hope at all. Who hopes for what they already have? But if we hope for what we do not yet have, we wait for it patiently. (vv. 23-25)

Jesus shows us a new way to be human. A new way to be human means there's a new way to be male.

TIME TO GROW UP

Purity culture framed our sexual virtue as something we have and then lose through sinful behavior. But centuries before sexual purity was a common way Christians spoke about this aspect of life, the church called believers to grow in the virtue of chastity,[8] which is the healthy and holy expression of our embodied sexuality that is self-controlled, joyful, and honoring of ourselves and others. Like all Christian virtues, chastity is not something we're born with and then try to keep. Neither is it a virtue only single people are called to grow in. Chastity is a calling for all Christians, one that we grow into more and more as we mature.

Those who are in Christ are in a lifelong process of growing up. We are meant to mature beyond our sinful brokenness. Here's the beautiful thing: our sputtering and imperfect performance is not a barrier to our acceptance by God. His love for us is underserved, but genuine. We are adopted into sonship with Jesus, an embodied male human being whose Father said about him, "This is my Son, whom I love; with him I am well pleased" (Mt 3:17). If you are in Christ, you, too, are God's beloved son or daughter, and he is well pleased with you.

Salvation doesn't end with forgiveness. The process continues with renewal, what many theologians call sanctification, the lifelong process of being made into new men and women. This is not just about learning rules or adopting a Christian vision for marriage and sex. It's about learning by the Spirit to become the type of humans we're meant to be. The gospel is about death and resurrection. Jesus' death secures our forgiveness and puts our broken humanity to death. Jesus' resurrection gives us hope for the renewal and resurrection of our own bodies.

The remainder of this book contains reflections and suggestions on what this renewal and redemption might look like, and how we can mature beyond our malformed and toxic masculinity. No Christian man should be defined by these traits, and in Christ, we don't have to be.

Enough is enough. It's time to grow up.

PART III

GROWING UP, BECOMING A MAN

EIGHT

BEFORE YOU KNEW
YOU WERE SEXUAL

BOYHOOD AND THE FORMATION OF MALE SEXUALITY

I'M NOT SURE EXACTLY WHERE THE IDEA CAME FROM, but I remember thinking often as an elementary-aged boy, *If I see a girl or woman naked before I get married, I won't be pure anymore. If someone sees me naked before I get married, I won't be pure anymore.* I believed I would have lost something forever that couldn't be regained. Even though I didn't understand what sex was or purity meant, I remember feeling the stakes were terrifyingly high.

My family of origin fits many evangelical stereotypes: white, suburban, six kids (I'm the fourth), homeschooled, dad at work, mom at home. One day when I was eight or nine years old, we hosted a gathering of other homeschooled families at our house. A handful of the moms were chatting in the living room, and I happened to walk past the living room on my way upstairs. I noticed one woman breastfeeding her child under a privacy cover. But while I was walking through, she rearranged herself and her baby. For the briefest moment, her breast was exposed through a gap in the cover—and I saw it.

I felt a rush of embarrassment and I hurried out of the room and upstairs. Then the thought hit me, as clear as day: *I'm not pure anymore.* My stomach twisted and I felt a panic sinking in. It's difficult to say whether I peeped on purpose. Boyish curiosity was a factor. I told myself it was an accident, so it didn't count. But I also knew I had lingered, that there was part of me that wanted to look. The moms hardly registered my presence. But their indifference didn't change the guilt and shame I felt. My little boy heart believed something terrible had happened—that I had let my parents and my future wife down, and that God now viewed me differently.

THE BEGINNING OF OUR SEXUAL STORIES

Male sexual dysfunction plagues the church and our culture. I want us to do better. And if you're reading this book, I imagine you do too. So, let's talk about growing up, becoming more whole and holy versions of ourselves, becoming the men we were created to be.

Growing up is not about becoming stronger, more stoic, a better leader, or more assertive. It's not about being sexually perfect or pure, suppressing your sexuality at the expense of your humanness. Instead, it is about becoming more like Jesus—more truly human. As Nathan Pyle writes, "Being a man isn't about being manlier; it is about being a man who is becoming fully human."[1]

A central burden of this book thus far has been understanding how male sexual dysfunction, abuse, and mistreatment of women and children have found a foothold in Christian communities. People don't become abusers out of nowhere. Even milder, subtler mistreatment of women is a function of our broken culture and errant teachings about masculinity and sexuality. Boys begin receiving toxic messages long before they hit puberty.

I'm neither a psychologist nor a therapist, so I'm not qualified to advance a complex argument about developmental psychology, but as Freudian and cliché as it may sound, the overwhelming consensus among experts in these fields is that our childhood experiences are formative for issues of sexuality. So rather than starting with adolescence when we awaken to our sexual selves, I'm beginning with childhood, in particular, boyhood.

STICK TO THE SCRIPT

Childhood is characterized by innocence and a sense of wonder. I see this in my son who, on our walk to his nursery this morning, stopped dead in his tracks to watch an excavator dig a trench for some new piping in our local park. I see it in the way he plays alongside me with his toy pots and spoons while I'm making dinner, the way he insists on helping me zest a lime. He's still mostly non-verbal, but he manages an earnest "Aww!" every time he sees the neighborhood cat, Fluffy, in the street.

Part of the innocence of young boys is that they're not encumbered by how they may or may not be living up to their culture's scripts of masculinity. Little boys don't know that—according to the arbitrary "rules" determined by our cultural context—pink is for girls and blue is for boys. My son doesn't know that he's expressing interest in a what many consider to be a "feminine" activity, preparing food, when he asks to help me with the lime. He's just living out of a sense of wonder and discovery.

I don't consider it a problem, per se, that our culture has categories for masculine and feminine. It's a natural outworking of the normative sexual binary. But Christians should think carefully about how they commend these cultural scripts to their children. Much of what is taken as a biblical standard for maleness is more cultural than it is Christian. For instance, it would be difficult to argue from the Bible that playing sports is a more masculine form of recreation than dancing—remember, King David was a musician and a poet, who danced with passion before the Ark of the Covenant on its way into Jerusalem.

Little boys start to learn these scripts from a very young age. My son is three years old. As his father, I am the primary model of masculinity in his life—a very sobering thought. It is the responsibility of Christian parents to filter these scripts through our Christian confession, to revise or reject aspects of cultural standards for masculinity not in keeping with the new world inaugurated by Christ's resurrection.

DISNEY PRINCES

What messages about masculine sexuality are boys receiving at a young age? Entertainment plays a significant role. For instance, many believe Disney princess stories form little girls to see romance and marriage as central to their identity. When girls have been reared on these movies, is it any wonder they start dreaming about getting married at a young age?

Less appreciated is the way boys are shaped by these stories. I made a similar point in chapter three about how male characters in many adventure and Disney movies can expect to find a swooning, beautiful woman at the end of their escapades. *Aladdin, The Lion King,* and *Robin Hood* are examples from my own childhood. A certain type of sexual conquest is baked into many of our stories and entertainment. Boys are formed to expect that if they act heroically, they will receive the attention of a beautiful women as a reward.[2] While references to sex are rare in children's stories, the romantic implications for little boys are loud and clear: be strong and heroic and you will never lack a woman's attention.

Although depictions of men in children's media are now more varied, those who grew up in the '90s and earlier often saw chivalry tropes in their entertainment. Women were helpless and eager to give out their affection to men who treated them with kindness or rescued them from danger. Plenty of boys reared on these films grow up to be men who are self-sacrificing, serving others without demeaning women. These genuine virtues encouraged by the slay-the-dragon-get-the-girl narrative should not be overlooked. However, the *expectation of* female affection is often only a hair's breadth away from a sense of *entitlement to* female affection. This sense of entitlement—to women's attention, affection, and bodies—is at the core of many toxic behaviors.

Relationships don't work like this. Women and girls are free to make their own choices. They don't need to adhere to your assumed narrative for how they should respond to your actions. Women can usually tell when men expect them to follow a script—and oftentimes, they don't find it endearing. I'm not saying that heroic, strong, or courageous types of masculinity are all bad. Far from it! We should encourage little boys (and girls!) to be courageous, to help those in need. Boys should grow up to become men who channel their embodied male advantage toward good and noble ends. However, strength and heroism should not be reduced to a mere transaction whereby men earn romantic and sexual favors.

THERE'S NO CRYING IN BASEBALL

Little boys are emotionally expressive, but they are expected to become increasingly stoic as they grow up. This cultural value is illustrated in a scene from the sports comedy classic *A League of Their Own*. Set during World War II, the film tells the story of an all-women baseball league, which was started when MLB players went overseas to join the war effort. In one scene, a coach named Jimmy Dougan (portrayed by Tom Hanks) berates one of his players after she miscues in the field (failing to throw to the cutoff woman) in an outburst that's equal parts comical and disturbing. Unsurprisingly, she starts crying.

Dougan is indignant. "Are you crying!? There's no crying in baseball!" The scene is played for laughs, and at the end of it Dougan is ejected by the umpire, some justice for the way he treated his outfielder. The joke of the scene is based on a cultural stereotype many of us had assumed: girls cry, and boys don't.

Little boys have a complex relationship with their emotions. They learn from an early age that expressing vulnerability is "girly." Sometimes, when they fall and hurt themselves, they find their parents and teachers are welcoming of their tears. Other times, they're told to "tough it out" or "rub some dirt on it." No crying allowed. When boys are rowdy in certain contexts, like sports, they are celebrated. When they're angry or having an emotional outburst in another context, like the classroom, they find their behavior unwelcome and strictly regulated. Rather than learning healthy ways to express their emotions, boys learn to suppress them. They learn that vulnerability is incompatible with cultural values of masculinity, which serves to cut them off from deep connection and life-giving relationships.

When they grow up, men and adolescent boys will sometimes express their deepest frustrations through sexual activities. Sex constitutes some of the most meaningful interpersonal connection men experience in their lives, but it can also serve as a way to act out suppressed dark emotions. Misogynistic comments, sleeping around, even coerced sex with his wife may be a man's way of soothing these feelings so he can feel "affirmed" in his masculinity. Men who struggle with sexual compulsiveness and addiction later in life are often nursing an emotional wound from childhood. When the dark emotions common to every person's experience are bottled up for years on end, they too often surface in dark deeds against women, children, and other men.

The complex emotional lives of boys are an important piece of male sexual formation and dysfunction. Even stoic men who rarely give outward shows of emotion would likely find, with the help of a counselor or therapist, that sex or the lack of sexual connection constitutes an emotional experience in their lives. Sexual sin is often the expression of an immature emotional self. And both well-regulated and poorly regulated emotional patterns almost always have roots in childhood.

FIRST EXPOSURE

In a sex-obsessed culture, portrayals of the sexual and erotic are everywhere. Sexualized mainstream entertainment is only the surface of a much deeper world of adult content, a world that children stumble or are intentionally brought into all too often. For some children, explicit and dehumanizing pornographic images are their first meaningful exposure to adult male and/or female nudity. Early exposure to pornography[3] and graphic sexual content intrudes on healthy sexual development. Prepubescent children will often have no context for pornography when they come across it. Oftentimes, the exposure will be covert, with friends or older kids.

Peter, one of the men I interviewed, described his first exposure this way: "I was actually scared. I had this sense that we were doing something really wrong, but other kids around me seemed unfazed by it. Other boys were doing things inside of their sleeping bags that made me very uncomfortable. I just rolled over and buried my face in the couch cushion until it was over." Peter concluded, "I wish there was some way I could go back and help my fifth-grade self avoid, or at least process, that stuff." Peter's empathy for his younger self is understandable. It makes me think of similar experiences in my youth, as well as my desire to protect my kids from uncomfortable and dangerous situations. I imagine many readers can relate to the confusing, even terrifying experience of sexual exposures that came too early.

Many Christian approaches to hypersexualized content in our culture has been to avoid and protect. I'm not saying that we should abandon this effort, but attempts to protect children are often combined with a "purity" paradigm that suggests preventing exposure is the name of the game. Yet, filtering software will never be able to keep up. Exposure will happen. So, we must do more than shelter children. We must also begin the lifelong work of forming their virtue.

Children are intuitive. Little boys can understand they wouldn't want other people looking at their private body parts without them knowing. Little boys can understand that giggling about someone else's body is disrespectful. Little boys can understand that women's and girls' bodies aren't theirs.

We can also destigmatize the human body by describing it in anatomically accurate ways. Using words like *penis* instead of *wee wee*. Or, for girls, this means talking not only about their vagina, but also their labia, vulva, and clitoris. It might include taking children to a museum with non-erotic portrayals of the human form that capture the dignity and beauty of human embodiment. For obvious reasons, I would hesitate to say we should intentionally expose children to nudity, but finding wise and appropriate ways to appreciate and teach children about the dignity of the human body is of the utmost importance.

Another factor to keep in mind is curiosity. Boyish curiosity is not evil. It is a good, God-given impulse that can drive us to understand and discover the beauty in the world. But curiosity can end in dark places. There's no perfect innocence in a broken world. We can't keep little boys pure forever, as much as we wish we could. Inevitably, to paraphrase Andrew Peterson, there comes a moment when we realize the world is broken and that we're just as broken as the world.[4] This is the plight of being a little boy—not only that he will face the brokenness of the world, but that he himself is broken and will actively participate in that brokenness.

Little boys need the gospel. Not the truncated gospel that only tells them that their sins can be forgiven. The full gospel that says they can be renewed and resurrected. That God wants them to be everything he created them to be.

THE ROLE OF PARENTS

Relationships with parents also play a key role in shaping boys toward healthy or toxic expressions of their sexuality. The sexual behavior you saw modeled by your father shapes you from an early age. Think back to what you observed. Was he openly affectionate with your mother? Did you ever see him viewing pornography? How did he look at and talk about women? Did you ever even see him interact with women other than your mother? Did he talk to you about women? Their bodies? Your body? Did you hear about, know about, or witness unfaithfulness on your father's part? Did he have children with other women than your mother? Did he express his feelings? Did you ever see him cry? Did he apologize when he was too rough or harsh with you?

What about your mother? Was she affectionate with your father? Did you ever get the impression she was afraid of him? Did she express her greatest care or concern about you when you did something wrong? How did she talk to you about your body? What about girls' bodies and women's bodies? In later years, how did she talk to you about relationships with the opposite sex and with the same sex?

Finally, there's the question of abuse—did your parents or parental figures treat you in ways that violated the fixed erotic boundary between parent and child?

If any of these questions brings up a noticeable reaction in you, that may indicate something worth discussing with a trusted friend, a therapist, or a pastor. Wounds from our fathers and mothers shape us deeper than we know, and they are often our first window into what sexual relationships might look like.

While I'm grateful for many things about my parents, I'll note one general thing that has been difficult for me about my upbringing in relation to sexuality. Both of my parents were adult converts to Christianity. After becoming Christians, they viewed the sexual permissiveness of the culture through a new lens. They saw the pain they had experienced in broken relationships and the regrets they carried from their own decisions. They wanted better for me and my siblings.

But this well-intentioned desire for my good was often motivated by fear—fear that I might make the same mistakes as their younger selves, and thus experience similar pain. As it turns out, my story ended up looking different from theirs, but I was not spared the sting of sexual pain. The fear my parents had about sexual sin translated into a fear of sexuality in general for me as a young person, a generalized fear and guilt that has been difficult for me to shake in adulthood. The culture of fear around sexuality is a common refrain of many who grew up in Christian homes during 1990s and 2000s. Others will have had different experiences with their parents, and I couldn't catalog all those dynamics and all their implications for adult sexuality. Still, your childhood relationship with each of your parents shapes you, and this dynamic needs to be included in a conversation about masculine sexuality.

ABUSE AND CHILDHOOD FORMATION

Abuse of children shouldn't exist at all, and it certainly shouldn't exist in churches and Christian communities. But it does. Several of the men I interviewed for this book told me stories of how their experience of abuse shaped them and their sexuality.

You'll recall Jordan's story from chapter five. His experience of repeated childhood sexual trauma pushed him toward violating others later in his life. For Jordan, the formational power of these experiences was never acknowledged. He was placed into one-size-fits-all accountability and sex addiction groups that didn't take his experience of abuse seriously enough.

If your earliest sexual experiences involved someone coercing you to look at or do something that you didn't understand or feel comfortable with, those experiences have shaped you. If the person who abused you is a man, this modeled a coercive and selfish vision for masculine sexuality.

Boys and men who have been abused tend to live in silence because of the unique stigma associated with being a male survivor. This is compounded by the spiritual abuse and retraumatization that often accompany sexual abuse in Christian contexts. Add to this the stigma against any same-sex eroticism in Christian communities. Since the overwhelming majority of perpetrators are men, most sexual abuse situations that boys experience are male-male.

Admitting to and facing this reality takes adult men to a place many of them don't want to go—the acknowledgment that they participated, willingly or unwillingly, in a same-sex sexual encounter.

Survivors of childhood sexual abuse need more than Bible verses and accountability, though these can be a genuine source of help, comfort, and healing. Survivors need love, relationship, acceptance, and—perhaps most importantly—good, trauma-informed therapy. The insights of the psychological community are gifts from God. If you are a survivor of abuse, I can't recommend trauma therapy enough. Therapy can—and for Christians, I would argue, should—be supplemented with Scripture meditation or memory, as well as embodied practices like mindfulness and physical exercise. For Christians, the path to healing should also include relationships with safe, empathetic, and well-informed mentors, pastors, and friends.

If we want to heal the wounds in ourselves, our sons, and our communities, we must acknowledge the reality of abuse and start bringing it into the light. We must create space where this can be discussed without shame, fear, or stigma. Too many men carry these wounds alone. And wounds like this can fester until they replicate. Those who do the wounding have often been wounded themselves as boys.

CONCLUSION

The seeds of toxic masculinity are all around us, and they take root in the lives of young boys. If you began to learn these toxic patterns as a child, the process of growing into a mature male will involve more than magically developing the willpower to stop watching porn or to end your extramarital affair. The path to healing and wholeness will involve unlearning the dehumanizing behaviors and messages that formed you into who you are today.

If you're a parent, teacher, or leader of some kind, you have an important role in shaping boys to be men who treat themselves and others—especially women—with the respect and dignity their humanity deserves. We can speak of the created goodness and glory of both male and female human beings. All people, all bodies, are good and worthy of respect—even if they don't follow our particular understanding of what men and women should be like—an understanding that, by the way, is often much more cultural than it is biblical. This universal dignity of the human person is a profoundly Christian principle, and it's one that even the youngest of children can understand.

Childhood—boyhood—is so important. It is a precious and beautiful season of life. Remember, Jesus loved children. He invited them near and rebuked the disciples for shooing them away. He understood they should be protected and cherished. We must likewise be committed to children's good and flourishing, and the fight against dehumanizing masculinity begins with them.

NINE

FROM FIGHT TO FORMATION
REFRAMING ADOLESCENCE AND SEXUAL TEMPTATION

DURING THE EARLY 2000s, every night sometime around 2:00 a.m., certain cable networks would switch over to a seemingly never-ending loop of *Girls Gone Wild* infomercials. These bizarre videos captured near-naked college-aged girls at drunken parties and pitted them in ridiculous games against one another, often involving water and mud. As degrading and dehumanizing as it was, the "girls" in these videos (never referred to as women) always appeared to be having a great time. The alcohol-fueled spectacle was an adolescent boy's fantasy: youthful and perky naked women tumbling over each other, delighted to flash their breasts for the camera.

My friends and I sat mesmerized watching these commercials during more than one sleepover. The tiny censoring boxes obscured just enough bare skin to make it legal to air. We were all good Christian kids, and we knew we shouldn't have been watching. But we didn't stop. We couldn't turn it off.

PORN AND THE CHRISTIAN MALE PSYCHE

I was having early experiences with masturbation and pornography in my tweens. By this time, I was already steeped in purity culture logic and rhetoric. I knew pornography was a grave threat to my soul, and sexual sin seemed like the worst kind of sin you could commit. But like many young men of my generation, I often sought out pornography as I grew into physical maturity. I easily bypassed accountability software on family computers, using an old iPod Touch that sat innocently in a kitchen drawer. I even used the janky web browser on our Nintendo Wii. I grew adept at finding covert ways to get to porn and hated myself for every second of it.

Some of you may be familiar with a similar struggle. On the one hand, your sexual upbringing has instilled in you the importance of sexual holiness, and you're certain your use of porn makes you desperately wicked and unable to be a faithful marriage partner. On the other hand, you feel powerless to avoid the urge to watch porn and masturbate—despite the gospel-centered teaching and resources meant to help you stay pure. The result is a split self, a separation between body and soul, which can lead to serious mental health issues and emotional distress.[1]

Here's the thing: porn is destructive. The solution to this problem isn't to shrug our shoulders and downplay its effects, saying "boys will be boys." Porn is bad. It's dehumanizing, both for its "actors" and users, and often acts as a gateway to untold amounts of sexually violent behavior in our society, not to mention the sexual violence and abuse involved in the production of pornography and the sexual violence it portrays.

But let's be honest for a second about the appeal of pornography. If you're a curious adolescent, the internet gives you unlimited, free, anonymous access to people who look any way you like doing anything you can imagine in any context you want. Past generations of the sexually curious couldn't have dreamed of this—any sexual fantasy come to life before your eyes. When adolescent kids are drawn to porn, we shouldn't be surprised.

Few Christians need convincing that watching pornography is wrong. Still, I wonder if it might be helpful to shift the way we talk about adolescents' porn use from moral compromise to moral immaturity. The compulsive use of pornography, both for adolescents and adults, often signals some unmet emotional or physical need. There is a spiritual dimension to a struggle with pornography, but the issue is often over-spiritualized. Porn use is often a symptom, not the disease itself. It is the way that a deeper issue of emotional repression and soul woundedness presents itself. As Jay Stringer writes, "The draw toward pornography does not indicate that you need to get your boxing gloves out for a heavyweight fight against lust. Instead, it may be revealing the latent pursuit of purpose in your life."[2] Sometimes habitual porn use can be an occasion for finding better coping mechanisms for dark emotions. This could be as simple as taking up a new hobby, going to bed at a decent hour, or some good old-fashioned psychotherapy.

I'm wary of two opposite ditches relating to pornography use and teenagers. An overemphasis on avoidance and moral disgust leaves vulnerable teen boys feeling alone and disgusted about themselves when they fall prey to pornography's seduction. But normalizing porn use normalizes dehumanization, leaving young people vulnerable to malformation and toxic sexual relationships later in life.[3]

Parents and leaders must be willing to enter the uncomfortable space of walking with teens as they navigate this especially difficult part of growing up in the modern world. Moral outrage is easy. Shrugging and letting kids do their thing is also easy. Walking in the space between these two ditches is hard and uncomfortable. For many kids, stern warnings aren't enough. Silence is even worse. And a bit of sympathy and understanding for scared, lonely, and ashamed teens with developing brains can go a long way. It would be hard to overstate the emotional agony young people experience around this issue. Yes, far too many Christian boys will watch porn as they grow up, but it's not necessarily the end of the world when they do. Many young men mature beyond this and go on to have happy and healthy sexual lives. I'm not saying pornography is no big deal or that we should turn a blind eye to it. Nor am I saying adolescent boys (or girls) should have free, unlimited, and un-supervised access to the internet. Like training wheels on a bike, safeguards are wise and appropriate as teens mature in their sexuality, and an empathetic presence can soothe like cool water in a desert of shame and isolation.

THE ETHICS OF PORNOGRAPHY PRODUCTION AND CONSUMPTION

Progressive Christian author Nadia Bolz-Weber has raised questions about whether the moral outrage around pornography use is always justified. She points out that while porn often leads to damaging effects in people's lives, like alcohol, it can be used in moderation and even be a mutually enjoyable experience for some couples. She also suggests there is such a thing as "ethically sourced porn" that avoids the toxic and dehumanizing aspects of much of the industry.[4]

What I appreciate about Bolz-Weber's approach is that she seeks to pastorally address the guilt so many men and women feel around their use of pornography. She doesn't want to drive people deeper into cycles of shame for something they already feel bad about. Where she and I part ways, however, is in the suggestion that porn use and production can ever be anything other than dehumanizing. This claim is not an exercise in picking "the low hanging fruit of moral outrage."[5] It's simply calling a spade a spade. Is pornography an ethically complicated and multi-faceted issue? In a sense, yes. But is it morally ambiguous? No. This is not about shaming people who already feel bad—and I know very well what it's like to feel guilty about consuming pornography. Rather, condemning porn is about defending human dignity, and here are a few reasons why.

Porn is non-relational. Sex and sexuality are about relationship. The capacity for pleasure and procreation written into our bodies has a purpose, a relational purpose that is bypassed in pornography. When we view pornography, we gratify ourselves with another person in a way that is separated from relationship with them and concern for their well-being. In this sense, porn is not like alcohol or food. When we overdrink or overeat, no other human being is directly involved in the act. Therefore, the moral logic of moderation does not apply to sex in the same way.

Porn is disembodied. In a similar vein, pornography short circuits the embodied aspects of our sexuality, teaching us that presence with another person's body is irrelevant to our experience of sexual pleasure. It reduces sex to content that can be sent, shared, or purchased like a meal for delivery.

Porn is often violent. There's a vicious cycle that few seem prepared to acknowledge between toxic masculinity and the ubiquity of pornography on demand. Porn gives the illusion of harmless indulgence in violent and degrading fetishes that diminish the human dignity of men, women, and children. It is the single most pervasive cultural factor in the radicalization of men and boys toward toxic male sexuality. A generation of boys reared on it have been given a false and unhealthy set of expectations for what a real, adult sexual relationship looks like. Not all porn would be easy to classify as violent, but the violence of the industry involves more than what happens in front of the camera.

Porn is non-consensual. The connections between pornography and human trafficking have been well documented.[6] And even in situations where someone consents to being filmed for porn, all you have established is that the production of the video was not illegal. But what about the sharing of that movie with strangers on the internet? Are the consumers confident the people who appear in pornography have consented to the production? And what about when consent is coerced? What about when it's withdrawn? The reality is that consent, what some claim should be the sole criterion used for sexual ethics, is almost impossible to establish in pornography.[7]

The common thread in all these aspects of pornography is dehumanization, which is sin. The shame many of us feel around compulsive pornography use is telling us something. It is signaling that pornography dishonors others and ourselves, that humanity is somehow being diminished, that there has been a fracture in our right relationship to the world.

As I've already suggested, the formative role of porn in our society should not be underestimated. A friend in high school once said, "All guys' sexual education comes through porn these days." There's a lot of truth to this. Many of us grew up with parents who were hesitant to talk to us about the details of sex. And where parents and educators are silent, pornography will step in and fill the gaps. Jay Stringer says, "When your parents abdicated their power to frame healthy and normative sex education for you, they were, intentionally or not, creating a world of silence and intrigue. Where parents and faith communities will not educate, pornography will."[8]

Christian books on sex often bemoan the unfair standard created by the youthful, peppy, full-breasted women that feature in so much porn. But the way women look in pornography is not, in my estimation, what's most problematic. The inaccurate sex education porn provides is much more damaging. For instance, boys are taught precious little in porn about how female bodies work, including the embodied realities of menstruation, vaginal lubrication, or the clitoris.

How are parents and youth leaders countering this pornified sex education? Usually through avoidance. Yes, we should encourage young men to flee from porn's seduction, like the wise father in Proverbs telling his son to flee the adulterous woman. But more important than protecting our sons from pornography is the way we engage boys when they do interact with pornography. Do we treat them with kindness, grace, and understanding? Or do we meet them with shame, fear, and disgust? Are we countering the toxic messages in porn with a good, accurate, and dignifying sex education? Do we give boys nuanced categories for thinking about their experiences and exhort them toward greater maturity? The fragile and unformed hearts of boys need more than condemnation. They don't need over-spiritualization. They need love.

MASTURBATION

The Bible says nothing directly about masturbation. But that doesn't mean we as Christians should have nothing to say about it. Can masturbation become an unhealthy habit? Absolutely. Is it usually accompanied by lustful thoughts? Yes, probably. But we should also ask what sexual thoughts count as lust. It won't do biblically or theologically to say the experience of sexual desire or sexual feelings are sinful, though the Bible does have a category of sinful sexual desire (Ex 20:17; Mt 5:27-28; Rom 1:24).[9]

The main issue when it comes to masturbation is, again, one of dehumanization. Masturbation becomes especially problematic when it means gratifying yourself with the thought of another person without their consent. Human beings should not be reduced to their utility for stimulating our mind's erotic inclinations. In this sense, masturbation is a dehumanization of others. There's also a strong theological argument to be made that masturbation falls short of the created purpose of mutual self-giving in sex. Masturbation takes what was meant to connect us to another person and bends it back toward self.[10] In this sense, masturbation could be considered a dehumanization of oneself. Many Christians throughout history have made this argument and continue to do so.

However, I do want to allow for some nuance and disagreement around masturbation. Many who definitively pronounce that masturbation is sinful are heterosexual married Christian leaders. One could argue that this is the easiest position from which to say masturbation is a sin, especially if you interpret 1 Corinthians 7 to mean that your spouse must have sex with you whenever you want. Most therapists and psychologists would describe masturbation as a normal, even healthy, human behavior. I'm not suggesting Christians should uncritically adopt every conclusion psychologists make. Psychologists aren't pastors, though some have pastoral and theological training. We should also acknowledge there is disagreement on the ethics of masturbation on both the theological side and the behavioral-psychological side of the discussion.

We ought to be careful about making far-reaching pronouncements about masturbation's sinfulness or non-sinfulness. I've read many books claiming one way or the other, but I sometimes wonder if such claims are helpful. If the Bible is our final authority, let's not go beyond what the Bible says and burden people with added rules (Mt 23:4). This can too easily translate into a denial of the created goodness of human bodies and sexual desire. Raising an adolescent boy who never masturbates is a tall order, and I fear setting this as the immediate goal for young men does more harm than good.

I am not suggesting Christians should disobey their own conscience about masturbation. I grant there are strong theological arguments to be made against the act. I have my own convictions about it that I have arrived at through reflection, prayer, and conversations with friends, mentors, and my wife. Personal convictions are fine; adding to God's law is not.

NOT *EVERY* MAN'S BATTLE

Titling a book *Every Man's Battle* is a stroke of marketing genius if you want to sell copies to, you know, every man. It plays into one of the myths of purity culture: that men as a group are hypersexual and have a difficult time saying no to sinful sexual desire.

Saying all men struggle with lust is like saying all men struggle with anger. Do a lot of men struggle with anger? Sure. But are *all* men angry? Imagine if a popular Christian book about controlling sinful outbursts of anger was called "Every Man's Battle." How would this affect the way Christians thought about men and anger? It would imply sinful anger is an essential part of being male. Some men do have anger problems; many men don't.

There's another problem with the title of this book. It frames the cultivation of sexual virtue as a fight, tending toward macho or violent stereotypes of masculinity. But not everything about being a man is about trying to kill something.

Many men don't spend their lives agonizing about and trying not to watch porn. Plenty of them simply move on with their day when they see a sexualized advertisement or a woman on the street wearing a low-cut top. They don't obsess over it. Lots of men have meaningful relationships with women, even women they might find attractive, without feeling tempted to undress them in their mind. Lots of young men know how to respect the girls at school and at their youth groups, including the ones they date.

Respecting women and controlling dehumanizing urges is not a radical concept that all men struggle to live out. The men who do struggle should have the support and resources for rehumanizing themselves and learning to think differently about other human beings. I understand the intention behind normalizing the struggle. But is a compulsive tendency to dehumanize and sexualize others something we want to normalize? I worry such blanket statements have become a self-fulfilling prophecy. They also signal to women that all men are dangerous closet perverts.

Saying lust toward women is "every man's battle" is unhealthy for at least three other reasons. First, the association between maleness and sexual desire leads men with low sexual desire to feel as if they aren't real men—and, conversely, it leads women who experience powerful sexual desires to feel as if they are unfeminine. Second, it causes boys to live in fear of their bodies and sexuality. And third, it directly excludes men who don't experience sexual desire toward women.

A DIFFERENT KIND OF BATTLE

For all the bickering among Christians around whether sexual orientation is a helpful category, it should not be controversial to say gay people are people. Nor should it be a stretch to point out that Christians have done harm to LGBTQ+ people.[11] A common form of harm is the simple refusal to acknowledge the presence of people who claim LGBTQ+ identity in Christian communities or saying they're not "real" Christians if they identify as such.

But LGBTQ+ people do exist. They are human and deserving of love and dignity. The overwhelming majority of boys who are attracted to the same sex first experience this attraction in adolescence and will continue to experience their sexuality as such in adulthood. Christian attempts to "convert" people to a different sexual orientation are at best misguided and almost certainly harmful and dehumanizing. I say misguided because this approach to gay teens misunderstands heterosexual desire as a necessary part of being Christian.

Differences of opinion exist on how gay Christians should express their sexuality, and these disagreements will likely continue. A problem I see on both the conservative and the progressive sides of this issue is the regular stereotyping of those who disagree, as well as a refusal to allow for the existence or religious sincerity of those on the other side.

Christian books on sex and masculinity often fail to acknowledge the existence of boys and men who don't fit into the Christian mold of heteronormative desire, which primes adolescent boys experiencing same-sex desire for serious struggle. This is a struggle for their very dignity as human beings, often translating to serious mental health struggles, even suicide. We must stop associating "true" manhood with the intense experience of heterosexual desire. There's nothing biblical to warrant this. And it does serious harm to all kinds of boys and men, both gay and straight.

REHUMANIZING ADOLESCENT BOYS

One Sunday during college I was in a car with some friends on the way home from church. I'm not sure how the conversation started, but I remember getting to the point where I was bemoaning my ongoing struggle with lust, porn, and masturbation. A couple of the guys in the car were in my accountability group at college, so it wasn't completely out of left field, though I've always been an over-sharer, which maybe doesn't surprise you after reading this book.

I remember feeling suddenly overwhelmed with shame and frustration that this was still a struggle for me. "I just really had hoped I would have this lust thing under control and figured out by now," I said, exasperated and holding back tears. "Sometimes I don't know what else to do. It won't go away."

There was an awkward silence, the kind that sometimes follows in male company after you express something vulnerable or talk about your feelings. Then one of my friends spoke. "Well, at least you're trying, right? I mean, you're working on it. You don't need to have it all figured out right now. Give it time and I'm sure it'll get better. You're a work in progress."

It seemed so trite, even annoying. If I was honest, it was hard to believe there would be a time in my life when I didn't consistently fight the urge to look at porn. But looking back, the advice I would give my younger self is exactly the encouragement that my friend gave me. Hang in there. Keep at it. God loves you. Formation doesn't happen overnight.

When I was thirteen years old, watching those *Girls Gone Wild* commercials, I don't ever recall thinking either I or the men producing these videos were dehumanizing women. I only knew I was doing something terribly wrong. The Christian message to sincere and struggling young men is often, "Hurry up and get your crap together before it eats you alive and ruins your future." But men and boys don't just need tough love. They need patience, kindness, and assurance that they aren't forever lost because of their sin and immaturity. Whoever you are, you are a good creature—broken and imperfect, yes, but created and loved by God. He is glad he made you as a sexual being. If you are in Christ,

TEN

YOU SAY GOODBYE, I SAY HELLO

DATING, ROMANCE, AND EXTENDED SINGLENESS

LIKE MOST TEENAGERS, I experienced a good amount of fear and trepidation around romantic relationships in junior high, high school, and college. Added to this was the high-stakes fear of sexual compromise drilled into me by purity culture. I had read all the books. I knew all about being "unequally yoked" with someone who didn't share my faith. I was even wary of Christian girls who hadn't been reared in the same purity-conscious corner of the subculture as me.

I took these ideals on myself. Ironically, I was more of an apologist for kissing dating goodbye than my parents, who affirmed some of the principles but didn't outright forbid us from any type of dating relationship. Still, like many white Christians my age, my experiences of young love were haunted by the feeling that romance was a trap set by Satan to ruin my life. My feelings for girls butted up against Joshua Harris's no-dating purity standards. One part of me obsessed about whether I could explore these connections in a way that honored God. Another part of me just wanted to be a normal teenager who experienced the excitement of holding someone's hand in the hallway, who could ask a girl to prom without feeling like I had compromised my faith.

Despite all this, I did end up dating a little during these years. One of these relationships was with Courtney.[1] A few months in, I came home with a hickey on my neck. I wore a collared shirt the next day attempting to hide it, but my mom still noticed. After inspecting my neck, she looked me dead in the eye from less than two feet away and said, "I am very disappointed in you." She had never said anything like that before. My dad folded his arms and shook his head without saying a word from across the room. The shame was astronomical.

While Courtney sometimes attended church, she didn't grow up in the same evangelical subculture of purity I had, which made my parents nervous. The next morning, they informed me I had to break up with her. I felt so guilty that I went through with it. I had a panic attack while talking with Courtney, but I knew I had sinned grievously. I needed to repent and return to my parents' good graces.

This was far from the end of it. We stayed broken up for a time, but forbidding adolescent romance has never been an effective strategy. Since before Romeo and Juliet, star-crossed lovers have been defying their parents' wishes. Courtney and I struggled for over a year to resuscitate our silly teenage relationship, our melodramatic brains filled to the brim with the emo music of the mid-2000s. But the relationship couldn't bear up under the constant weight of shame I felt about it, not to mention the ongoing tension with my parents. The cycle eventually broke. I "recommitted my life to the Lord" and broke it off with Courtney for good, framing myself as the hero of the story and her the villain. My stomach turns when I think about the ways I mistreated her, particularly by overspiritualizing our breakup.

HYPERSPIRITUALIZED ROMANCE (OR LACK THEREOF)

Rachel[2] was another of my quasi-romantic relationships. She *did* grow up in the same faith subculture as me, and ironically we bonded over our shared purity ideals. We felt safer getting close emotionally despite the supposed dangers of opposite-sex friendships. This relationship was also emotionally tortured. Remember, I had been conditioned to think girls were a barrier between me and God, so when I (unsurprisingly) developed feelings for Rachel, I interpreted this as a spiritual battle. At this point, I was reading books by Elisabeth Elliot, the widow of famous missionary and martyr Jim Elliot. Books like *Passion and Purity* and *Quest for Love* were both hyperspiritual and romantic, even sensual.[3] In these books and others, romantic attraction—even between two Christians—was seen as a dangerous and powerful force that could negatively affect your relationship with God.

Admitting I had feelings for Rachel would have amounted to moral and spiritual compromise. But when I couldn't take it anymore, I told her my feelings—with all the melodramatic self-pity and self-righteousness I could muster. I told her I needed to cut off our friendship and focus on my relationship with God. As hyperspiritual and ridiculous as it seems now, I thought of this as a spiritual test, like Abraham's test in Genesis 22. In my mind, God was seeing if I was willing to give up my friendship with Rachel for him. I was trying to prove my spiritual worth, all the while secretly hoping God's reward for my sacrifice would be a rich and meaningful future love story with Rachel (like he did with Jim and Elisabeth Elliott).

Rachel was not impressed.

After several months of not talking, my few interactions with Rachel were awkward. She told me I had hurt her by cutting off contact. I believe her exact words were, "What the hell was that? That was the shadiest thing anyone's ever done to me in my whole life." Our friendship sputtered out after that. We never dated, but for me the ordeal was accompanied by the emotional weight of breaking off a years-long relationship.

I take no pleasure in telling these stories. It's more than a little embarrassing. Purity culture sought to simplify life for teenagers by sparing them all the emotional and spiritual consequences of dating. But instead, it complicated romance for me. My temperament, emotional immaturity, and skewed views about relationships caused me to mistreat both girls in big and small ways.

Some of my Christian friends, exposed to the same purity teachings, seemed better able to navigate anti-dating rhetoric. They had relatively normal romantic relationships, including ones that didn't cross the horrifying boundaries we were told so much about. I didn't have sex before I got married, which was one of the goals of purity culture. So, mission accomplished, I guess? But the emotional weight of these and other relationships was amplified by the high-stakes purity rhetoric.

"BIBLICAL" ROMANCE

This book is not another dating manual. But, in context of our wider discussion of male sexuality, we may still ask the question: How should Christians date? In short, in a way that dignifies each person as a human being. We should honor, respect, and affirm the beauty of each other's maleness or femaleness in ways that are in keeping with the new humanity that is coming to be in Christ.

The Purity Movement exchanged one culturally situated model of romance (dating) for another culturally situated model (courtship), which Harris advocated for in his follow-up book, *Boy Meets Girl*. However, it would be difficult to argue that the Bible teaches courtship as the model for finding a spouse. Is courtship what happened with Ruth and Boaz, for instance? As a widow and a foreigner, Ruth and Naomi were in a precarious situation. Naomi saw Boaz was able to make that better. Together they shrewdly used the cultural categories of romance and matchmaking available to them to make the marriage happen. Ruth and Naomi were the instigators of this match. It was not a courtship agreed on by Ruth's father (or Boaz's). The book of Ruth is not a crosscultural manual showing us God's way to find a spouse—it's just a culturally situated love story.

The Bible includes wisdom about human sexuality, but it is not an exhaustive how-to book for your romantic life. Part of the trouble with the last couple decades is we've said too much about romance and called the advice Christian. So, instead of detailing another overly specific, dogmatic approach, I offer a few broad principles based in Scripture and theological convictions.

Start with human dignity. The New Testament refers to men and women in the Christian community as brothers and sisters. A key instance of this language appears in 1 Timothy 5:2, where Paul charges young men to treat "older women as mothers, and younger women as sisters, with absolute purity." This is a reminder that all of us in Christ are a family. The word here translated "purity" is *hagneia* and is related to the word for "holy" (*hagios*). The language of holiness recalls that all who are in Christ belong to God. Humanization, love, and concern for well-being are at the heart of this metaphor. Christians should resist totalizing others in terms of their sexuality, and we should resist the urge to manipulate others for our own selfish ends.

Sexuality isn't just about sex. Fear-based rules around opposite sex relationships run the risk of "effectively reducing the totality of human sexuality to brute sex."[4] Our sexuality does more than drive us toward pleasure and reproduction. It signals that we, as humans, are not complete in and of ourselves, that we need each other for community and friendship. It drives us to reach out to people in love for connection. It reminds us that God is communal, three in one. Loving relationships with others extend beyond the courting of marriage partners or the erotic intimacy between spouses. Even those who believe sex ought to be reserved for marriage should remember sexuality isn't "turned off" until they get married. We should bear all this in mind as we move toward others for relationship. A date may not result in a marriage, but that doesn't make it a waste of time.

Dating and romance can lead to pain and heartbreak—and that's okay. Many regulations around dating are born out of a desire to avoid negative consequences and heartache, but the fact that we may experience pain in dating is not reason to avoid it. *All* relationships involve the possibility of risk, even heartbreak. We may experience some level of regret about choices we made in and around relationships, but the fear of future regret is not a reason to close ourselves off from romance. There's no secret formula that will protect you from heartbreak—that's not how life works. And being willing to risk some vulnerability is exactly what love is. As we move deeper into love, we move deeper into vulnerability. This is what God's movement of love toward us in Christ looks like. Jesus' love for us was not self-protective; he made himself vulnerable even unto death (Phil 2:6-8). This doesn't mean teens and young people should foolishly throw themselves into unhealthy relationships, but wisdom should be balanced with the recognition that all relationships are messy in their own way. Just because dating can be complicated and painful doesn't mean it should be avoided.

Wise parents and mentors should have an age-appropriate role in romantic relationships. Purity culture placed a strong emphasis on the role of parents in guiding and regulating their children's dating and courting relationships. There is obvious, biblical wisdom in this (Ex 20:12; Prov 1:8; Eph 6:1); teenagers have no idea what they're doing. It's true that authoritarian parenting can sometimes push young people toward the very behaviors parents want them to avoid—I've seen this play out in many people's lives, including my close friends. But this doesn't change the fact that rules and boundaries are important for children, even essential. It's also essential that these be supplemented with a wise, loving, patient, and empathetic presence. Moreover, grace and forgiveness should permeate the entire process between parents or mentors and kids. We all fall short in many ways.

Boundaries matter. How far is too far? The most classic youth group question. How much physical affection can we get away with while dating without sinning or ruining my future marriage?

Early in my relationship with Shelby, I remember having conversations about boundaries for our physical affection. We decided together that we would save our first kiss until we were engaged. (The first-kiss-at-the-altar standard commended by some Christians seemed a little extreme, even to us. Shelby and I were happy to settle for purity culture's silver medal.) At the time, it felt like the God-honoring thing to do and was in line with much of the teaching I had received and books I had read. Looking back now, it all seems a little unnecessary, even bizarre. But that doesn't make creating a boundary wrong. Mutually agreed-on boundaries are important in any relationship, including marriage. Talking about them is an important way of respecting each other and establishing consent while dating and beyond.

Thinking back to her experiences in youth group, my friend Julie, whom I've already mentioned, wished the conversations had taught boys and girls to ask permission before doing things, not just setting up boundaries to make sure they didn't have sex. She also noted that "sex" wasn't even defined. It was just something they shouldn't get close to. To make sure you don't get close, it's better not to kiss or even touch each other all. For those who decide together they'd like to hold off on sex, having boundaries in place may be a very good idea. That said, purity culture took a wise practice to an extreme. Intense restrictions around things like holding hands, hugging, or a kiss goodnight made teens that much more obsessive and frustrated. It didn't give kids space to enjoy and explore age-appropriate physical affection. A mutual crush of mine in junior high youth group once apologized for giving me a hug to say goodbye. She wasn't apologizing because I hadn't consented to the hug; she was apologizing because she had violated a purity culture norm.

So, what can we say positively about boundaries? Here are some guiding principles:

1. Start with human dignity, which is the logical foundation for consent.

2. Remember that physical affection is about connection, not recreation.

3. Greater intimacy will tend toward greater vulnerability, which will naturally incline us to desire more intimate forms of affection—and that's how it's supposed to work.

4. The level of commitment should correspond to the level of physical intimacy.

This final principle undergirds the historic Christian teaching that sex should be reserved for marriage. It is at least reasonable that the greatest acts of physical intimacy correspond to the greatest level of relational vulnerability and commitment. The point, in my view, is not to save everything possible for your wedding day or soon after. It's to make sure, in your own conscience, the physical intimacy you pursue and invite is not out of balance with the level of your relational commitment. Additionally, for those who continue to believe the Bible requires extramarital abstinence, the matter is one of obedience to God.

Dating isn't practice for divorce. One of the common refrains of purity culture was "guarding your heart" for your future spouse. The implication was that creating a romantic connection with a person you didn't end up marrying made you less able to commit to a lifelong relationship in the future. This bit of purity culture advice backfired badly. Not breaking off a relationship that should be broken off can itself be a recipe for divorce. You know what's worse than a practice divorce when you're dating? An actual divorce after you marry a person you shouldn't have. Julie put it this way: "I think the church has often pressured women to stay in toxic situations. Purity culture isn't the only reason for that, but I've seen friends stay in both dating relationships and marriages that are abusive because they felt breaking it off would compromise them for the future." Julie went on to tell the story of a good friend who was sexually assaulted on her first date with a Christian guy. The friend didn't tell anyone about the assault, and she felt pressure to stay in the relationship because of purity culture standards. She ended up marrying her assailant. Unsurprisingly, this was not a happy marriage. He abused and beat her, and the relationship ended in divorce.

People with sexual histories are not damaged goods. Remember the flower passed around the room at youth group until it's all janky and disgusting? Or licking a lollipop and asking if anyone else wants to lick it? These were meant as purity culture mic drops, but the illustrations always felt off to me. I never thought, *I could never be with a woman who had been with another man.* I thought, *If I really loved her, I don't imagine I'd feel like this was a big deal.*

I understand people bring sexual baggage into their marriages, but someone with a sexual history is no less valuable as a spouse. The damaged goods narrative is a disgusting, sub-Christian, and often misogynistic idea that has no place in the Christian community. It infuriates me that the church cultivated this view of human beings and virginity, not least because my wife is a survivor of childhood sexual abuse. The suggestion that I or anyone should view her as somehow less worthy of love and connection fills me with a unique type of rage. Damaged-goods rhetoric stems from a commodification of marriage, with virginity being a gift for your future spouse.[5]

MARRIAGE AS AN EVENTUALITY

Let's return briefly to a point from chapter two. Renewing our view of dating in the church involves repenting of our idolatry toward marriage. Getting married is seen as having "arrived" in the mainstream Christian subculture. Singleness, then, is viewed as a life stage on the way to the full humanity found with marriage and family. I hope what I said about Jesus in part two of this book shows why this is problematic. Christianity is a religion with a single, chaste, and childless Savior.

Marriage isn't an eventuality. It's a possibility. Singleness is more than a stopping point on the way to the marriage God has promised you. For some, singleness will be a lifelong way of being human. Extended singleness has its challenges—but so does marriage. Instead of being helped toward Christian maturity as single adults, men are often told to hurry up and get married. There's nothing wrong with wanting to marry, but the evangelical church has often done a horrendous job of dignifying singleness itself.

There are also those lesbian, gay, and same-sex-attracted Christians who make the difficult choice to live according to a traditional sexual ethic. For these believers, lifelong celibacy becomes a calling of Christian faithfulness. They shouldn't be destined for a life of loneliness and second-class status in churches, and the Christian message for them isn't that God can turn them straight. Is it any surprise LGBTQ+ people find many church communities to be difficult, even hostile spaces? Perhaps the reason some are threatened by the presence of queer people in church is that we have idolized the institution of heterosexual marriage as the apex of human flourishing. The problem may not be sexual minorities' erotic inclinations as much as the church's failure to cultivate communities that actually take the Bible's picture of Christian kinship seriously.

Our desires for sex remind us that so much of human life is about connection. It's about desiring others and being desired ourselves. Finding a partner for a sexual relationship is a profound and powerful expression of this desire for connection, but it is far from the only way we express it. Desire for connection is baked into everything about what it means to be human. As Curt Thompson writes, "Every baby comes into the world looking for someone who is looking for him or her."[6]

If we conceive of Christian community as consisting only of children, parents, and adults who are on their way to heterosexual marriage, we have suffered a serious failure of imagination for what an inclusive and life-affirming community can be. Too many churches cast no vision for long-term single adulthood and offer no clear articulation for how opposite-sex friendships can be a part of it.

Luke is a single Christian man in his thirties. When I interviewed him about his experiences in the church, he told me, "For a while I lived in this narrative where I felt excluded because I was single, and it was easy to feel sorry for myself. But more recently I've realized that, as a single person, I'm empowered for relationship in a way that married people aren't. There's a lot I have to give that's unique." Luke faces certain struggles as a single person, but he is also especially well positioned to give and receive love from others because of his singleness. The journey into Christian love is by no means limited to marriage, and the journey toward full humanity is not limited to the journey to find a spouse. As Thomas Merton, a Catholic monastic priest, wrote, "We do not become fully human until we give ourselves to each other in love. And this must not be confined only to sexual fulfillment: it embraces everything in the human person—the capacity for self-giving, for sharing, for creativity, for mutual care, for spiritual concern."[7]

We will talk about marriage in this book, but it's critical to remember that not everyone gets married. As we move through the stages of a man's life, we must remind ourselves that marriage is not the endgame. All men, young and old, married and unmarried, should aspire to something greater than finding and keeping a wife. We should aspire to mature, whole, healthy, virtuous expressions of our sexuality.

ELEVEN

ACT LIKE AN ADULT

MATURING THE CHURCH'S CULTURE OF MASCULINE SEXUALITY

DURING COLLEGE, SHELBY ONCE WORE a sleeveless dress while volunteering as a worship vocalist in church. If you're a woman who grew up in purity culture, you know where this is going. One of the church elders expressed concern to the worship pastor that Shelby was "causing the men to stumble." The dress was neither low cut nor short; the issue was her exposed shoulders. Without speaking to Shelby, a woman in the church was asked to rush home and get a cardigan sweater for Shelby to wear during the second service. Before the service began, Shelby was ushered into a back room by this woman and two elders. The woman told her she was distracting men in the congregation and needed to wear the sweater for second service. Shelby was mortified. She began sobbing and the men awkwardly left the room while the woman stayed to help her regain her composure.

Shelby was never asked to serve on the worship team again. Despite having no ill intent, Shelby was made to feel she was the problem, and she was forced to accommodate to men's sexual perception of her.[1]

DEHUMANIZATION AND ACCOMMODATION

Some men think they don't objectify women, simply because they've shunned bikini posters, *Game of Thrones*, or porn magazines.

However, the church elder who eyes women up and down to determine whether outfits are modest enough has also reduced those women to sexual objects. This isn't to suggest it's appropriate for women to dress provocatively at church, but if the men can't stand to see a bare shoulder or two on a hot summer day, the women are not the issue.

This is just one example in a broader culture of dehumanization. It is not as pronounced in every church or community, but in a post-#MeToo and -#ChurchToo world it is something every Christian man and leader should take seriously. Allegations of abuse and misconduct are often dismissed; women bringing accusations are seen as hysterical or jealous for influence; youth pastors are fired for sexual misconduct in one church only to be rehired by another; patriarchal systems of leadership and authority create abusive systems of power.

Many women understand these dynamics, but men are often less aware of it. The sad reality is that conservative Christian churches are one of the easiest places in American culture for a power-hungry and abusive man to mistreat women and children while commanding the respect of the broader community. We have made our churches comfortable for abusers. Shall our churches continue to be shelters for oppressors rather than the oppressed? May it never be! Our churches must become hostile to unrepentant abusers.

Christian men need to grow up—and I don't mean they simply need to be braver, bolder, take responsibility, lead their families, move out of their parents' basements, play less video games, or woo a woman and get married. I'm calling Christian men, single and married, to become more Christlike in the way we think about, treat, and live in relationships with women.

Too often the church has presented marriage as the solution to immature masculine sexual tendencies. But men who objectify women will continue to do so, whether or not they are married and able to enjoy marital sex. Not all men marry, and the ones who do marry have no guarantee of becoming sexually mature individuals. Relationships are not a crutch for our dehumanizing sinful habits. We need to reframe and mature our vision of masculine sexuality in order to reform church culture.

A CULTURE OF SEPARATION

As soon as boys and girls are old enough to have sexual self-awareness, church ministries often sort them into sex-specific spaces. Boys are shuffled off to talk about porn and not looking at boobs, while girls spend their time talking about eating disorders and how to cover their boobs. This is a bit of a caricature, but not completely. Separate women's and men's groups are also common in adult discipleship. Entire ministries are built around sexual segregation, and ministry staff structures often split pastoral roles for men's and women's ministries. I'm not suggesting we completely abolish this practice. I do, however, want us to consider how this sexual segregation affects our individual and communal formation.

Sex-specific ministries can become problematic for multiple reasons. First, they can communicate that the only legitimate reason for men and women to mingle is so they can pair off into couples and create families. Second, they can signal that men and women can never be trusted to share space without falling into sin. Third, the activities of these segregated groups too often conform to gender stereotypes. Guys get together to eat bacon and watch football. Women get together for tea, crafts, and mothering seminars. What about men who don't enjoy sports? What about women who don't have children? There are whole swaths of people that don't conform to gender norms—and I'm confident lots of women like bacon.

This segregation isn't just about discipleship ministries. Often, women are excluded from meaningful leadership in churches. Many have an all-male ministry staff accountable to an all-male elder board. Women are not invited to meetings or asked to give input, and female leadership positions are often reserved for children's and women's ministries. The church is deprived of the voices and gifts of women, and children's ministries are deprived of the important influence of men.[2]

(NOT SO) VIRTUOUS PASTORS

The culture of a church often conforms, for better or worse, to the character, competencies, and vices of its senior leaders. If we hope to address the toxic culture in many of our churches, it's important we start with the pastors.

I've heard many male pastors speak at length about their moral guardrails—accountability software, never spending one-on-one time with a woman other than his wife, not watching R-rated movies, not going to the beach or gym, and so on. What does this communicate to the women in the congregation? Something intended as a display of integrity may make people feel that all men are either actively participating in or could easily fall into sexual sin.

Men in America are not inclined to broadcast vulnerability. We don't like admitting to physical weakness, emotional instability, embarrassment, or depression. However, sexual sin is an area in which Christian men are sometimes happy to broadcast weakness. I noticed this in the wake of the 2021 Ravi Zacharias news: pastors and sincere Christians saying, "If I'm not careful, that could be me."

Why do we tolerate this in male pastors? Yes, humility is important. And we do well to heed Paul's warning, "If you think you are standing firm, be careful that you don't fall!" (1 Cor 10:12). However, I worry we've given special allowance for Christian leaders to be regularly enticed by sexual sin. We think this is normal because it's part of the adolescent masculinity we've adopted in the Christian subculture. But imagine if we normalized ongoing vulnerability to other kinds of sin? What if a pastor admitted to regularly being tempted to steal things, gamble away his family's earnings, or punch people in the face? Would we describe this as normal male behavior? We expect Christian leaders to habitually say no to these vices—even without rigorous accountability parameters.

In an earlier chapter, I talked about my own porn use as a Bible college student. The hard truth is that, though I aspired to pastoral ministry, I was not qualified to serve as a pastor while struggling with compulsive porn use. We shouldn't compromise on this, as challenging as the ubiquity of porn use among young Christians may be. If you're a pastor or an aspiring pastor, habitual porn use or any other sexual compulsion is a serious concern, one you should not minimize.

I'm not trying to shame pastors for being sexual beings with sexual desires. But if you are teetering on the edge of sexual scandal, please, for the good of yourself and your congregation, get some help. You don't have to live with the constant struggle. I'm not saying there won't be difficult moments or days or seasons. I'm not saying that temptation will never come and never be enticing. But the daily grind of constant enticement to sexual sin is not what Christian maturity looks like. There's too much at stake for you, your family (if you're married), and the congregation you serve. Your unwillingness to deal with the brokenness in your heart could have eternal implications in the lives of your congregants. If you need help, get help. It's a matter of spiritual life and death.

I can't say it better than the apostle Paul: "Watch your life and doctrine closely. Persevere in them, because if you do, you will save both yourself and your hearers" (1 Tim 4:16). Pastors bear a sober responsibility of tending to their own attitudes and behaviors toward women, as well as the conduct their teaching perpetuates in the wider community. The call of Christian leadership requires sexual maturity. God will judge pastors more strictly; if you're a pastor, God will judge you more strictly (Jas 3:1).

HOLDING ACCOUNTABILITY ACCOUNTABLE

I'm in favor of accountability and guardrails. However, if we're not careful, certain forms of accountability, like web-blocking software, can be counterproductive in cultivating self-control. Purity culture often focuses on creating *external* regulations for people's behavior. When the community is overly rigorous in enforcing purity standards and people's behavior is controlled *for them*, it deprives them of the opportunity to learn to *control themselves*.[3] A pastor should be well-practiced and regulated in controlling his sexual urges. If the only devices he ever uses are locked up with accountability software, what happens when he suddenly has access to a computer or phone without them? He will be unpracticed in the normal, healthy adult habit of not looking at porn every time he feels the urge.

For many men, accountability groups continue to be a decisive piece in their growth toward wholeness and maturity. However, a repeated refrain in my interviews for this project was the ineffectiveness of small group accountability. This is admittedly anecdotal, but bear in mind that these are men actively trying to stop unwanted sexual behavior. So, why have men sometimes found these groups less than helpful?

Accountability groups can go wrong in several ways. First, while their stated goal is often to encourage vulnerability and authenticity, they can also incentivize cycles of self-withholding, even lying. It's hard to be authentic when doing so feeds a negative narrative of self. Everyone wants to be doing better than they are, which leads us to deceive ourselves and then deceive others about the extent of our sin.[4]

Another pitfall of accountability groups is that they can sometimes normalize sexual sin. There's comfort in knowing someone else is facing similar challenges and understands your struggle. This is the genius of Alcoholics Anonymous. However, if we're not careful, this logic can normalize dehumanizing sexual behavior. Recall Chris's comment after realizing his friends also struggled with lust:

"I didn't think they were so bad, so maybe I'm not so bad either." In one sense, this is a good and freeing realization. In another, it can easily slip into a minimization of unhealthy and immature habits, creating a culture of license around compulsive sexual behavior.

Finally, accountability groups can unhelpfully narrow our vision for discipleship. Peter, one of my interviewees, told this story: "I got into a small group once, and all the guys wanted to talk about was lust and sexual sin. I tried for a little bit but realized this wasn't going to work for me. I wanted to read the Bible, I wanted to dig deep into the Scripture." Peter wanted more from his discipleship group than a weekly confession of sin. There's a place for weeping over sin together, but the question is whether and how we move beyond these feelings. Too many accountability groups serve only to drag men down together into cycles of deeper shame. Another man put it this way, "I remember in college joining these groups where men would just talk about lust and sit around hating themselves for it. I feel like that's exactly what Satan would want. It didn't feel like a place where the Spirit was at work to grow us into better men."

So, what steps can we take to hold accountability groups accountable? First, remember that authentic community is about relationships, not just accountability. Peter described another time in his life following a breakup where he fell deep into compulsive use of pornography, viewing it several times a week. When I asked him what helped him out of this phase, he said that it was a close friendship with two other guys. "It was just friendship. I suppose I was lonely, which was why I was struggling with porn so much. I felt valued by these guys, and we talked about all sorts of things. It wasn't an accountability group—our conversations about God and theology helped pull me out of the pit."

Another way to form healthier accountability groups is to consider having more mature Christians present to encourage, empathize, and share wisdom. Believers should be in relationships with other believers who they can aspire to be like in the future. When everyone in the group has the same ongoing struggle, there can be a failure of imagination for what Christian men can and should be. Accountability is not a silver bullet for our sin and brokenness. Relational accountability is just one step. We should also check in with ourselves and others on whether the accountability is working. Is it helping us grow in holiness? Or is it leading us into greater self-deception and isolation? Accountability should involve deeper questions than whether we've done anything unsavory in the past week, which tends toward performative righteousness, not matters of the heart. Deeper questions about fears, desires, acceptance, and shame will go a long way into making us feel known. Many men may find this uncomfortable to start, but it's the type of accountability and connection many of us need.

IS COMPLEMENTARIANISM THE PROBLEM?

Since this chapter is about church culture, let's talk about an elephant in the room for a moment. Isn't all this toxic masculinity the result of complementarian theology? Complementarianism is a reading of the Bible that understands men and women as equal in dignity but distinct in their roles in the church and the home. It also understands men to be the biblically prescribed leaders of both the church and the home. The complementarian view of gender "roles" is the standard position of many conservative evangelical churches and denominations in America. It's not hard to see the *possible* connection between sexual abuse and an ideology teaching that God has given men authority over women. So, is complementarianism the cause of Christian toxic masculinity? It's complicated.

A disturbing pattern has emerged in recent years. Those who defend, cover up, and tolerate abusive behavior often appeal to a woman's need to submit to men in authority over her. Women are forced to stand by husbands who mistreat them and their children. Husbands get off with slaps on the wrist from all-male elder boards when the situation warrants a criminal investigation. Women's voices are routinely silenced, excluded, or dismissed as overly emotional or less biblically informed. These dehumanizations are often associated with complementarian teaching. For example, the ministry of Mark Driscoll was characterized by strict and outspoken complementarian ideology. *The Rise and Fall of Mars Hill* podcast clearly demonstrated this church culture was deeply dysfunctional, toxic, and abusive for women. Moreover, the negative experiences of congregants and ex-staff members were often dismissed and minimized for the sake of the ongoing "health" of the institution.

Correlation is not the same as causation, but the association should get our attention. It's true that not everyone who espouses complementarian ideas holds active dehumanizing attitudes toward women, and many women report thriving in complementarian communities. Complementarianism exists on a spectrum, with some applications egregious and oppressive and others appearing to take seriously women's dignity, freedom, and flourishing. We shouldn't paint with broad strokes, but it's worth asking whether systems built around complementarianism tend toward the dehumanization of women.

Like the Purity Movement, complementarianism is culturally situated. The term itself was coined relatively recently by a group of pastors and Christian leaders, including John Piper and Wayne Grudem.[5] But the idea of male headship is not new and has been the dominant position in Christian communities throughout the world. Defenders of complementarianism understand themselves to be continuing in the church's long-held tradition, arguing that the view is rooted in the clear teaching of Scripture (Eph 5:23), even though many well-trained, faithful, and orthodox scholars would disagree with such a claim.[6] I have my own opinions, but I'm also still in process. I feel it's appropriate for those (like me) who grew up in complementarian contexts to sit and listen to those speaking out and rebuking us and our churches.

Belief in male headship does not require embracing the toxic, patriarchal form we have seen in recent history. But it should be beyond dispute that abusive patterns of masculine sexuality have found a place to thrive within complementarianism. If this wickedness can be rooted out from the broader system, these pastors and leaders should pursue solutions for their communities with all haste.

IS EGALITARIANISM THE SOLUTION?

Egalitarianism is the opposite theological position to complementarianism. It affirms women's ordination and usually denies the existence of biblically prescribed gender roles for the home. So, are egalitarian churches free from toxic masculine sexuality? The short answer is no.

Bill Hybels, formerly of Willow Creek Community Church, was an early and outspoken proponent of egalitarian theology in evangelicalism. As Hybels prepared to retire, allegations of domineering leadership and sexual misconduct came to light. At first, the church denied these allegations. Hybels was the widely beloved founding pastor, and the timing of these accusations was destabilizing for the future of a church facing such a significant transition. After a long and painful process, which included the resignations of Hybels, the entire elder board, and the female pastor chosen as his replacement, it was determined that these allegations were "credible."[7]

We're oversimplifying the problem if we think converting everyone to egalitarianism will solve it. Theological positions on gender roles and female leadership are relevant to these conversations, but let's not be so naive as to think a simple assent to the question of female ordination will make this subcultural sickness go away.

As the Hybels and Driscoll stories both illustrate, the protection of power and institutions is also at play. There's more to purity culture than abstinence and marriage. It also includes maintaining an appearance of purity for the organizations and systems that employ so many and "do so much good" for the kingdom of God.

CULTIVATING A CULTURE OF DIGNITY, ACCOUNTABILITY, AND FRIENDSHIP

We must replace dehumanizing teachings and practices with those that dignify women. This includes the way pastors speak from the pulpit, as well as the rules and advice presented on how men and women should interact. We must take seriously allegations of sexual abuse. We must heed the biblical call to elevate the plight of the oppressed, including abused and mistreated wives. We must remove the weight of shame from women who have been beaten, abused, or cheated on and place that shame where it belongs—on the men who harm these women.

Jesus said if a man looks lustfully at a woman, he has already committed adultery in his heart (Mt 5:28). He did not say, "Therefore, never look at women." Nor did he say, "Women, make sure men don't look lustfully at you." The responsibility remains with men to look at women differently. We must remind men that all women are worthy of dignity and respect because they are human—not just because they are someone's daughter, wife, or mother. A woman isn't valuable only because of who she is in relationship to a man. Though it can be helpful to remind men they should treat all women like family, a woman is valuable ultimately because she is a human being created in the image of God.

Christians must also create layers of accountability where men answer to the church community and society at large for how they treat women. A powerful aspect of the #MeToo movement was the way many women demanded their abusers be held accountable. This impulse toward accountability is resonant with the Christian principles of justice and protection of the oppressed.

We've often misunderstood the Christian call to forgiveness. Forgiveness does not mean withholding punishment and shielding abusers from legal accountability. Nor does it mean that predatory youth leaders are allowed to stay in ministry, or that women should be encouraged to stay with their abusive husbands, or that children should continue to spend time with their pedophile fathers. We must take sin seriously. Too often, when we say we're forgiving someone, we're sweeping sin under the rug to preserve harmony, balance of power, and a façade of peace in the community. True redemptive forgiveness cannot function without proper systems of accountability.

A pastor who needs blocking software to not look at porn or needs the Billy Graham rule to avoid sexualizing interactions with women is, quite simply, not fit to be a pastor. God isn't paranoid or afraid of false accusations. God values the actual integrity of his leaders, not the mere appearance of integrity. If our hope is in God and not our institutions, we'll be able to face the communal and financial disruption that will come if we hold leaders accountable. Let's believe women when they say they have been sinned against. Let's include women in the process of disciplining church leaders. This is the good, just, and righteous thing to do.

Paul writes in Galatians 3:28, "There is neither Jew nor Gentile, neither slave nor free, *nor is there male and female*, for you are all one in Christ Jesus" (emphasis mine). This is not a denial of the existence of ethnic or gender categories, but an insistence that the social barriers separating us from one another have been transcended by our oneness in Christ. The second-class status afforded to women throughout the world and across history ought not be represented in Christian communities. This is not merely a secular feminist impulse; it is a Christian one.

Christian men should also relearn how to be in meaningful, nonsexual friendship with women. Many people have close opposite-sex friends during high school and college. However, this is sometimes less true for Christians, who are socialized from a young age to view the other sex as threatening. Chris, a friend I've already quoted several times, admits, "I don't think I really had any platonic friendships with women. Because I had so sexualized the female body, I only pursued friendship with girls I was interested in dating."

When you know someone well, you often enjoy spending time with them. You understand their fears, desires, and passions. It is more difficult to reduce them to an object or view them as a threat to your purity. The hard social split between men and women does not serve our communities well. It does not form men to view women as friends and sisters, and it continues to fuel a narrative that men and women should be afraid of one another.

A few years after my wife and I got married, we invited Joy, a recent college grad from our church, to stay in our condo's guest room while she looked for an apartment. A few weeks later, her college roommate Janae also started staying with us. After a few weeks, at our invitation, Joy and Janae decided to stop looking for another place to live. We were a unique household: a married couple, their two-year-old daughter, and two single women. Our living situation raised some eyebrows. It seemed like something out of a sitcom. Since Joy and Janae were our peers in age, some people in our church expressed concern about the wisdom of the arrangement. Others assumed the reason they were in our home was to help with childcare, an assumption none of us appreciated. But as time went on, we four adults developed a true and deep friendship unlike anything else we had experienced. And I managed to maintain healthy relationships and boundaries with the four females sharing my home. I knew which one was my daughter, I knew which one was my wife, and I knew which ones were my friends. It wasn't complicated, and it was a rich and beautiful experience, one each of us continue to cherish.[8]

Sharing a home with Joy and Janae gave me opportunity to continue to mature my understanding of what it means to live in relationship with women. Our friendship was nonsexual but intimate. I knew many of their struggles, and they knew mine. Their presence in our lives was not viewed by either Shelby or me as a threat but a blessing. I learned from them. Shelby and I supported them and they supported us, both as a couple and as individuals. To this day they are known and loved by our children.

The living arrangement lasted two years until it was ended by the pandemic. We've all moved on to different things, but the love that we have for one another remains. It's not a love that exists in spite of our sexual differences, but one made stronger and more meaningful by them. It was a source of joy and healing for each of us. For me, it was a way God continued to form and grow me toward mature expressions of masculine sexuality.

BE THE CHANGE

Grown men are responsible for their ongoing sexual immaturity. Think again to the example of Jesus. Did he avoid friendships with women? Did his ministry involve criticizing women's clothing or life decisions? Did he question the integrity of women or treat them like they were out to get him? Did he suggest that loose women were a plague to society?

The path toward restoring the dignity of the men and women in our communities does not involve denying our sexual selves. Far from denying our humanity, we must grow up into it. Yes, we must act like men, but before we can do that, we first need to act like adults.

TWELVE

THE WORST SEX YOU'VE EVER HAD

HONEYMOON HYPE AND THE IDOLIZATION OF MARRIAGE

SHELBY AND I WERE VIRGINS WHEN WE GOT MARRIED. Neither of us had been "tainted" by other sexual encounters, so we expected our first days as husband and wife to be characterized by beautiful and innocent discovery.

Then our wedding day came.

It was like a lot of wedding days—a mix of stress, excitement, nerves, and emotional and physical overload. The wedding night and the honeymoon were . . . fine? I mean, there were some good chocolate-covered strawberries in the honeymoon suite. And the cruise we went on was great. But the sex was bad. Very bad. And not the laughable bad of inexperienced lovers. It was a difficult, joyless, and disappointed bad, created by the pressure of the moment, repressed trauma, and unrealistic expectations—"the singular melancholy of the virgin's wedding night."[1] There was confusion about pain, an awkward visit with a cruise ship doctor, a feeling that we should be enjoying sex but finding everything else about the honeymoon more enjoyable.

Unpacking everything that made our first sexual experiences difficult would take a while, but there were two primary things going on. For Shelby, repressed sexual trauma from early childhood caused her body to dissociate during sex. It was impossible for her

THE WORST SEX YOU'VE EVER HAD

to stay mentally present because her body was communicating to her mind that she was in danger. She went into survival mode. We wouldn't understand this until years later. As I'm writing this, I'm sitting in our living room across from her. I asked Shelby how she would describe her early experiences. She responded matter-of-factly, "It hurt, and I didn't like it. I hoped if I kept doing it, it would hurt less. I felt like I was supposed to do it, that I had to do it."

For me, internalized shame from my upbringing and sexual education made me feel guilty about having sex, like it was wrong for me to enjoy it. This residual shame translated into an inability to enjoy my bodily responses. I had learned over the years to hate my sexual body. Purity culture had given me the impression that my difficult-to-control urges were the worst thing about me. When I got married, I found it wasn't just masturbating that made me feel guilty. Orgasms in general triggered shame. I always felt I had done something wrong, or that there was something wrong with me for experiencing pleasure.

GETTING OFF THE HYPE TRAIN

Some people who are virgins on their wedding night have beautiful early sexual experiences. But this is far from the guaranteed outcome some were led to believe. I have met an alarming number of people who saved themselves for marriage and found early sexual experiences painful, confusing, frustrating, or simply difficult for any number of reasons. Disappointing, even traumatic first-time sexual experiences have become something of a trope of evangelical memoir.[2] A Christian couple I know, Walter and Alice, once shared about their own experience. After having sex for the first time on their wedding night, Alice immediately started sobbing. Alarmed, Walter asked her what was wrong. She replied through the tears, "I thought it was going to be magical!" They were both cracking up when they told this story, but I don't imagine it felt funny at the time. In the system of purity culture, virgin-only honeymoons were hyped up as a euphoric sexual ecstasy. Mine and Shelby's was anything but. The honeymoon hype train carried us deeper into shame and confusion.

To be fair, many purity culture resources do their best to temper expectations about sex early in marriage. They commonly advise taking it slow and giving yourself time to figure it out. But I heard these sentiments alongside statements like, "Think how amazing your honeymoon will be!" For instance, I remember a sermon anecdote about how being snowed-in on your honeymoon was no problem because you could just have a bunch of sex. Looking back, I feel the lower-your-expectations advice was good, and the honeymoon hype was mostly unhelpful.

For the first five years our marriage, we didn't realize Shelby's regular indifference and hesitance toward sex was cause for concern. We had both been socialized by Christian culture to believe female reticence was normal. Still, her lack of enthusiasm only heightened the sense that I was wrong and dirty for having a sexual body with sexual desires. But our understanding of 1 Corinthians 7's teaching to "not deprive each other" made us push through, which only deepened our sexual dysfunction.

These days, Shelby and I both tell engaged couples who are waiting for marriage to drastically lower their expectations. We tell them our story. If sex clicks for them early, even on the wedding night, I'm delighted for them. But if it doesn't, I don't want them to feel alone, confused, or worried there's something wrong with them. Sometimes that's just how it goes—and that's okay! One friend told me a few weeks after his wedding that my advice was the most helpful thing he and his fiancée heard in all the months they were engaged. It helped him to not feel alone and gave them space to work through the sexual struggles they experienced in the months that followed their wedding.

It's time for Christian leaders and young people to get off the hype train. Stop telling unmarried virgins that honeymoon sex will be worth the wait. As I've already suggested, there may be good reasons for holding off until marriage, but mind-blowing wedding night sex is rarely one of them. Oftentimes, serious sexual struggle can linger long after the honeymoon. Honeymoon hype sets young people up for disappointment. Disappointment sets people up for disenchantment, marital dissatisfaction, infidelity, even losing their faith. Concern for kids' sexual and spiritual lives motivated the Purity Movement, but the tragic irony is that sexual and spiritual health have often been compromised by purity culture's rhetoric. Decades on, the movement has, for many, accomplished the opposite of its intended goals.

SO . . . WHY WAIT?

My intent in this chapter is not to advance an argument for why people should or shouldn't wait until marriage to have sex. Whether you take a traditional stance on premarital sexual ethics or not, I hope we can agree that the way in which purity culture commended abstinence until marriage was harmful. Premarital abstinence did not translate into hot, shame-free, and frequent sex for my marriage. Far from being a wonderful part of our lives, sex was and continues to be a consistent source of mental stress and emotional pain.

Purity culture sold us a bill of goods, namely, great marital sex and a harmonious marriage. We were told this was the reason to wait. Again, as Christine Gardner has said, purity culture used sex to sell abstinence. Far from challenging the broader culture's preoccupation with sex, Christians often encouraged us to idolize and romanticize it as a central part of life satisfaction and fulfillment.

So, I ask again, why wait? If someone's abstinent only because they think it'll result in a good return on their investment, they may be gravely disappointed. When our materialistic and sex-obsessed reasons for staying abstinent fall flat, what are we left with? We are left, on the one hand, with an appeal to "the Bible says so"—perhaps not a bad argument for those who adhere to scriptural authority— but people need to understand the *why* of this teaching if it's going to sustain them through difficult circumstances. On the other hand, we can appeal to the Christian tradition. The overwhelming majority of Christians in most times and most places have commended sexual faithfulness within marriage and chastity outside of it. This is part of historic Christian identity. If a professing Christian wants to part ways with this tradition, they are of course free to do so. Sometimes there are good, biblical, and gospel-motivated reasons for disagreeing with tradition. However, when we part ways with most other Christians on any given issue, we would do well to examine ourselves closely to see if we can in good conscience come to terms with this point of disagreement.

The point remains that people who found sex disappointing, those who never have been married, those who experienced divorce in their twenties, those who weren't able to "pray the gay away"—many of us were left asking what it was all for. Can the moral reasoning of premarital abstinence even stand up on its own? Too often the beauty of the traditional sexual ethic has been reduced to its effectiveness in securing future sexual blessings. So, what makes the traditional ethic good and beautiful? We'll return to this question one more time at the book's conclusion. For now, I'm content to sit with the tension and acknowledge the pain of those who were let down or harmed by the lies of purity culture.

THE IDOLIZATION OF MARITAL SEX

Sex does not make your life complete. Purity culture, like many patriarchal movements in world history, fetishized virginity and turned it into an identity.[3] Sharing your first sexual experiences with your first and only spouse will not heal the pain of loneliness and longing in your life.

One man I talked to, Bobby, told the story of a time he and a few other male students shared a cabin with their youth pastor at a retreat in high school. The pastor talked at some length about how "incredible" having sex with his wife was, how he couldn't wait for the boys in the youth group to experience their own sexual joys in marriage when they grew up.

This story plays into the idolization of marital sex as an experience that will make you whole, make you pure, make your wildest dreams come true. In this frame, marital sex is your savior, not Jesus. But marital sex is a false savior. It won't save you from your sin or take away the urge to sexualize others, masturbate, or watch pornography. I've heard more than one man say it's harder to resist temptation as a married man. One said "it takes less imagination" to picture yourself with another woman when you know what sex is like.

Your husband or wife will never be everything you dreamed for sexually. No person—no matter how beautiful, loving, selfless, or committed to your good and your pleasure—can bear up under the weight of all your sexual needs and expectations. If you expect them to be so available and open to you that you never again experience sexual frustration, they will disappoint you. That's not their fault; it's yours. You've made marital sex into something it was never meant to be. Your spouse can't be your god.

Virginity is not a "precious gift" you give to your spouse, or a means of securing their loyalty and devotion. This, again, frames our morality in terms of an idolization of marriage. Some go farther than demanding virginity from their future spouse. Chris recounted a casual conversation with peers at college. A friend of his said she couldn't marry a guy who had ever watched porn. Chris thought to himself, *Well, that excludes me and just about every guy I know.* The trouble with over-hyping virginity and sexual purity as a gift is that it makes non-virgins and the not-so-pure feel less valuable to their spouse. This is not a Christian way of thinking about human beings. It again leans into a dehumanizing cultural impulse that reduces people to their sexual status and utility. If marriage is about a loving covenant and self-sacrifice, let's stop making sexual satisfaction one of the terms and conditions of the contract.

DON'T GET MARRIED JUST BECAUSE YOU'RE HORNY

I went to Bible college, a subcultural context where it's still considered relatively normal for nineteen-year-old college students to get married a few months after meeting each other. I've already said it in this book, but it's worth repeating: 1 Corinthians 7 does not teach that horniness is a good reason to get married. It doesn't mean that any couple who experiences erotic angst should get married regardless of their life circumstances, maturity, and relational health. This is more sexual idolatry. Sure, some people who get married at twenty so they can have sex go on to have healthy and happy marriages. But too many others who get married for this reason end up divorced before long. Jordan, whose story you'll remember from chapter five, said he and his first wife felt they needed to get married to honor God because of their lack of self-control. This marriage was sexually dysfunctional from day one and ended in a messy divorce.

For the sake of illustration, let's take this popular interpretation of Paul's words to its logical extreme. Many fourteen-year-olds are quite capable of "burning with passion" for their boyfriend or girlfriend. Would we recommend they get married as soon as possible? Of course not. We tell horny teenagers to be responsible, keep it in their pants as best they can, be patient, and grow up a bit before making rash decisions.

On the flip side of this issue, others delay marriage too long. Rightly interpreted and applied, Paul's words in 1 Corinthian 7 are quite relevant for contemporary dating relationships. Many people delay marriage and commitment long after settling into sexual relationships, cohabitating, and integrating their lives. The culture has idolized financial security as a prerequisite to commitment. The dream of a perfect house, career, and marriage is much more American than it is Christian. Every culture has standard practices around the timing, age, and circumstances of marriage. The continued delay of marriage in American society (particularly among wealthy, well-educated whites) may betray a diminishment of respect for the institution of marriage itself. It's not obvious to me that "figuring yourself out" and "enjoying your twenties and thirties" are perspectives on life that Christians should uncritically adopt. Marriage is good, and delaying commitment is not always wise. People who love and care about each other shouldn't hesitate to commit to each other's good for a lifetime.

GROWING INTO INTIMACY

Many people feel sex in your twenties is as good as it gets. Young, perky, fit, bodies are what "good" sex is all about. The reality is that the sex young people have is often superficial, awkward, and, um, brief. (Sorry guys.) People who have been married for a while may say there's something charming about the early days, weeks, and years of their sexual relationship, but the best stuff doesn't come until much later. For example, Richard, a friend of mine who's been married for decades once told me that he and his wife didn't hit their sexual stride until their midforties, over twenty years into their marriage.

Honeymoon hype, fetishization of virginity, and idolatry of marriage are destructive. On the one hand, this approach to relationships ostracizes and stigmatizes those who are not virgins at the time they are married. On the other hand, it creates a false expectation of sexual ecstasy for honeymoons and early marriage. Good and fulfilling sex doesn't just happen if you follow a certain formula. For those who have been victims of trauma, sexual intimacy may be especially difficult. Marriage, and life in general, is about much more than sex. And growing into greater sexual intimacy isn't all fun and games. Sometimes it's frustrating. Oftentimes, it's hard work. So, in chapter thirteen we're going to talk about what sex in marriage is really like, and how men can learn to love and serve their wives well in this aspect of their relationship.

THIRTEEN

LEARNING TO LOVE

REFLECTIONS ON MARITAL SEX

A FEW YEARS INTO OUR MARRIAGE, I found myself being drawn back into pornography. This came at a time when Shelby was feeling unwell for weeks and unavailable for sex. I didn't know what to do with my pent-up energy, so I struggled and grew bitter. All the teaching I received as a single man held out marriage as the solution to my sexual frustration; I didn't know how to deal with this type of sexual frustration *in* marriage.

I sought out a conversation with my pastor. He listened, sympathized, and told me matter-of-factly and without judgment that I had been hypersexualized. He didn't tell me to get greater accountability or memorize more verses. He told me to go to therapy, to do the hard work of digging into my soul and my story. I needed to understand the pain that made me vulnerable to the dehumanizing allure of pornography. It was these conversations with a therapist, in conjunction with more open communication with Shelby, that finally led me toward consistent freedom from pornography. I'll repeat myself and say that therapy is not a silver bullet for all life's problems. It proved decisive for me in this season, but even after this first stint in therapy, I had more work to do.

Toxic masculinity is all about male entitlement—to power, space, freedom, preference, and pleasure. We associate sexual entitlement with Hollywood producers, frat boys, and "incels."[1] Men like Harvey Weinstein and Brock Turner are easy to villainize as the essence of what is wrong with men in our culture. But rather than throwing stones at others, Christian men would do well to examine themselves.

Too often the misinterpretation and misapplication of biblical passages are used to create and sustain a system of female sexual subservience and male sexual entitlement in Christian marriage. In 1 Corinthians 7 we find the countercultural exhortation that the body of a married man belongs in equal measure to his wife as hers does to him. Paul prohibits married men and women from depriving one another, but we shouldn't interpret this to mean a partner can never say no to sex. There are legitimate reasons for turning down a spouse's sexual advance. A wife is not in sin if she's not in the mood or too tired or unwell. Nor is she obligated to "take care of him in other ways" when her body doesn't allow for vaginal intercourse. None of these are a willful deprivation.

What is Paul talking about, then? The exhortation not to deprive one another fits into his larger point that sex in marriage should involve mutuality. When sex is used as a weapon or in only self-gratifying ways, marital intimacy is no longer about love, connection, and serving the other. It is about power and holding something over your spouse. But this passage isn't only addressed to women. Are there ways men deprive their wives of a mutually satisfying and self-giving sexual relationship? Men would also do well to ask themselves why their wife doesn't want to have sex with them when she turns them down rather than demanding their "rights." This Christianized version of male sexual entitlement continues cultural patterns of patriarchal dehumanization that do serious harm to both men and women.[2]

PURITY CULTURE AND PORN STAR WIVES

My expectations for marital sex were shaped by the teaching of Mark Driscoll, who was known for his frank, even graphic, discussions about sex. These were often grossly skewed toward male desires, fantasies, and gratification. More than once he joked about how a wife hesitant to perform oral sex on her husband repented when she realized, per Driscoll's teaching, that such servicing of her husband was "biblical." When asked about frequency of sex in marriage, Driscoll said that even when couples are together multiple times a week, many men are taking care of themselves three to four additional times on the side. The clear implication is that if a man's need for sex isn't fully satiated by his wife, she isn't meeting his needs in a biblical and faithful way.[3]

In late high school and early college, I was a Driscoll fanboy. I watched his sermon series on sex and marriage as a single, clueless nineteen-year-old. Driscoll's branding appealed to immature young Christian men like me. If you're horny and sexually frustrated, what's not to like about a hypersexualized Christianity that promises you erotic paradise in marriage? If you're a married man who would like to be having more sex, what's not appealing about hearing that blowjobs, stripteases, and sex three or more times a week are biblical commands?

To be fair, there's nothing unbiblical or unchristian about spouses enjoying oral sex, frequent sexual activity, or erotic dress-up. But it becomes problematic when we imply these are biblical commands or ways wives must honor and serve their husbands. A friend once told me their church regularly offers a seminar on sex specifically for women, titled "Light His Fire." All this suggests a male-centric view of sexuality not dissimilar from the worldview on display in mainstream pornography. What about getting your own fire lit, ladies? What if there are other ways to love men than being their sexual servants? Being sexually submissive to your husband at the expense of both his and your humanity isn't serving him in the long run. Oftentimes, it may simply be perpetuating and solidifying his sexual immaturity.

The pressure and expectation for constant sexual availability is one of the most damaging elements of widespread pornography abuse. It accustoms men to expect sexual gratification when they like in exactly the way they like without navigating the beautiful and complex realities of life and relationship. The women in porn are always a few clicks or taps away. They are enthusiastic, never tired, never pregnant or menstruating, always up for anything. Real women aren't like this. If you're a man who grew up on or continues to be formed by porn, you need to be continually unlearning this lie. When Paul tells married believers not to deprive one another, this does not mean wives should be as available as the pornography on their husband's smartphone, or that they must service him whenever he has a sexual thought.

Both pornography and purity culture left me ill-prepared for the times my wife wasn't receptive to sex. I could feel and act entitled without being demanding. I could feel wronged when stress from work or simple bodily limitations made Shelby less enthusiastic. This you-owe-me attitude is toxic, and it's something many Christian women deal with in their marriages. It dehumanizes a wife, the very woman a man is called to love as Christ loved the church. It reduces her humanity to her sexual utility.

REHUMANIZING YOUR WIFE

A husband should make sure he isn't putting his wife in a box prescribed by the Christian subculture or his own sexual preferences. Because of the cultural, physical, and sociological privileges associated with being male, men's sexual preferences can become dominant in many marriages. Christian teaching has perpetuated stereotypes that men are commanding and assertive and that women are docile and submissive. This is a recipe for a dehumanizing and imbalanced sexual relationship focused on the man's needs and the wife's duty. It makes couples that don't fit the stereotype feel they are somehow outside of God's will. Personalities and libidos vary considerably within the genders. Not every man should be expected to conform to the virile, assertive, and hypersexual model. Not every woman is sexually restrained, shy, hesitant, and passive. Women have desires, preferences, and thoughts about how they would like their sex life to work, but many men suck up all the sexual air in the room with their neediness and intensity.

What would a different approach to marital sex look like?

Maybe start here. Ask your wife, "What would you like our sex life to look like, irrespective of my preferences and desires?" Don't be overbearing. Be curious together about her sexuality. What sort of frequency sounds exciting? What types of foreplay? What time of day? What sounds relaxing? What sounds intriguing? What sounds safe? What sounds edgy?

Some women will have ready responses to these questions; others will find it difficult to come up with answers. That's okay. You're starting a conversation. The possibilities for how such a conversation could go are endless. Here's why: your wife isn't a mere participant in the stereotypes associated with female sexuality; she is an individual with her own story, hopes, and fears. Get to know her sexuality, so you can love and serve her better. This may involve giving her space and setting aside some of your own preferences and desires.

Many Christian men are compassionate, giving, and understanding lovers, serving and caring for their wives well. Too often this isn't the case, and our discussions around masculine sexuality in marriage revert back to fulfillment and entitlement. Thomas Merton writes:

> Love is not a matter of getting, and certainly not a matter of getting what you want. Quite the contrary. The insistence on always having what you want, on always being satisfied, on always being fulfilled, makes love impossible. To love you have to climb out of the cradle, where everything is "getting," and grow up to the maturity of giving, without getting anything special in return. Love is not a deal, it is a sacrifice.[4]

Healthy, loving marital sex is not about getting what you want. As Christine Emba writes, a sexual ethic focused on concern for the other person may well mean we have sex less often.[5] Men should ask themselves questions like, Am I overbearing? Do I account for my embodied advantage in the way I interact with my wife both in sex and in conversations about it? Do I tend to my own emotional needs in healthy ways? Or does my wife have to sexually babysit me every time I have a bad day? Does she have anywhere near as many orgasms as I do?

Mutual orgasm shouldn't necessarily be the goal of every sexual encounter; a fixation on orgasms can become a barrier to satisfaction and emotional intimacy. Still, there's something significant about the fact that men and women don't tend to orgasm the same way. It means that sexual intimacy is an embodied conversation of love, service, and sacrifice. If we're talking about orgasms, sex is not automatically mutually satisfying. Sex requires ongoing bodily communication, like a dance. Men, it can't just be about your needs. Sex doesn't work that way. A couple's dance can't be one-sided.

On a related note, compulsive masturbation and pornography short circuit the soul-shaping communication and dance of sexual relationship in marriage. As Jay Stringer writes:

> Pornography is appealing because all that is required is to show up feeling defeated, angry, lustful, or entitled and be promptly served any erotic content you desire. In pornography there is no one you must encounter in your ongoing struggle with premature ejaculation, no pain in not being chosen by a partner, no one who will ask you for emotional engagement, and no one who will hold you to account for having endured the distorted desires of your heart.[6]

Your relationship with your wife shouldn't be like your relationship with porn. This approach denies you the opportunity of growing into a more mature and fully human self. Mature sexuality means being relationally present, not treating your partner like a tension release valve. Healthy sexuality means being able to have sexual thoughts, even experience arousal, without feeling this entitles you to sexual release.

Be the kind of husband who finds joy in bringing his wife to orgasm and expecting nothing in return. Be the type of man who doesn't make his wife's orgasm about him, his performance, or his need to satisfy her. Be the type of man who joyfully does housework and childcare because it's the responsible thing for a husband and father to do—not so your partner will "reward" you with sexual attention later that night. It isn't all about your sexual needs and desires. Let there be times when it's about her needs, sexual and otherwise, and your duty to love her well.

SEX CAN BE WONDERFUL, BUT IT'S NOT EASY

This chapter may read like I'm being hard on men, or that I don't want men to have fulfilling sex lives. I'm as much in favor of passionate, exciting, frequent, fulfilling sex as the next guy. What I'm not in favor of is men assuming sex on their terms is what constitutes good sex.

Sex can be a wonderful experience. But rarely does this type of fulfillment and satisfaction come naturally, easily, or consistently. Author bell hooks writes,

> False notions of love teach us that it is the place where we will feel no pain, where we will be in a state of constant bliss. We have to expose the falseness of these beliefs to see and accept the reality that suffering and pain do not end when we begin to love."[7]

Learning to love is a process, and sex in marriage involves sacrifice, not just fulfillment.

Neither is healthy marital sex all about frequency. Kevin and Amber are a young Christian couple who, after a few years of marriage, found themselves settling into a less frequent sexual rhythm. They wondered if they were sinning because they didn't have sex more often. It was consistent, just not as often as they had been led to believe was healthy. Neither of them was unhappy, nor did they feel as if they were especially vulnerable to temptation because of it. Eventually, through wise counsel, they were released from the strictures of Christian expectations about sexual frequency. Kevin was able to relax. He no longer felt like less of a man for not wanting sex more. Amber was also put at ease. She no longer felt she was failing Kevin or exposing him to temptation.

There's nothing wrong with wanting to improve your and your partner's sex life. Christians should feel free to delve into the beauty and mystery of marital intimacy. We're well-served by the work of many Christian therapists and psychologists who study this topic.[8] Sexual dynamics can be some of the most complex aspects of life as a human being. Our sexuality and sexual instincts make us, in a way, like other animals. We are instinctively, even animalistically, drawn to one another by our biological wiring. But our sexuality isn't simply an instinctual urge. It's also a relational, spiritual, and transcendent part of ourselves. It draws us into vulnerability, intimacy, and pleasure of connection unlike anything else in our experience. Human sexuality exists at the intersection of body and spirit.

GROWING INTO MATURITY

We often think singleness is about sexual self-restraint and marriage is about sexual fulfillment and satisfaction. This is not true. Marriage, too, involves sexual self-restraint—lots of it. This is because marriage is about love, not gratification. Our marriage vows are about serving our spouse, not being served by them. Marriage is not a sexual transaction; it's a covenant of love and faithfulness.

What Christian marriage books don't always tell you is that, as you get older or as life circumstances change, you might have less frequent sex. You might have to deal with that like an adult instead of using it as an excuse to indulge in sin. No one wants to hear that sex may become more difficult, less frequent, and less satisfying in some seasons and circumstances. But this is just how it goes. The natural rhythms of menstruation, pregnancy, childbirth, and breastfeeding aren't the only interruptions you will experience in your sex life. New jobs, loss of energy from age or illness, work stress, work schedules, travel, emotional breakdowns, erectile dysfunction, taking care of children, in-law visits, resurfaced trauma— all of these and a million others will create challenges for your sexual relationship. That's okay. That's expected. Be present to your wife's physical and sexual needs, including when she needs space from you sexually. Remember, you are called to love her as Christ loved the church. And Christ did not come to be served, but to serve and give himself up.

Marriage is not always a sexual paradise. Sometimes it feels like as much of a sexual desert as abstinent singleness. This too is an occasion for growth toward maturity. It's not a stroke of bad luck that I married a sexual abuse survivor. A tragically high percentage of all women are survivors. Rather, it is God's grace to me that I married a woman who was unwilling and unable to be sexually available to me in the ways that pornography, Stephen Arterburn, Mark Driscoll, and a poor interpretation of 1 Corinthians 7 led me to expect. My experience of sexual intimacy is difficult, but I can't begin to express how thankful I am for the way this has forced me to grow up and grow into a more mature understanding of sex and my own maleness.

FOURTEEN

FATHERHOOD

THE CHIEF END OF MALE SEXUALITY

THE OVERTURNING OF *ROE V. WADE* sent shockwaves through American society. Many celebrated what they considered a hard-fought victory for the dignity and humanity of the unborn. Others saw the decision as an alarming step backward for women's rights. It's difficult to think of a political issue more polarizing, and my only commentary is that the issue of abortion comes down, again, to questions of dehumanization.

Feminists and abortion rights activists decry unjust systems of power around reproduction and sex. These are important and weighty issues. American society is embroiled in debates about female identity, particularly the close association of femaleness and female sexuality with children and childrearing. When Christians have waded into these debates, they have too often demonstrated the same dehumanizing patterns we've traced in this book and reduced women to their sexuality. Women are not machines for growing and taking care of babies, and female bodies don't create babies on their own. So how do men fit into this equation?

WHAT IS SEX FOR?

Our sexuality is not the totality of our identity. However, we would do well to ask what the sexual part of ourselves is for. An obvious possible answer is that our sexuality is for procreation. But very often male sexuality has been divorced from fathering children. The conception of a child is not a woman's capacity alone; it is a *shared* capacity of male and female human beings. Thus, it stands to reason that caring for children is an equally male and female responsibility. When women unfairly shoulder this weight, the solution isn't to disassociate feminine sexuality from motherhood. The solution is to reassociate male sexuality with fatherhood. If sexuality as a whole is disassociated from parenthood, who ultimately suffers? Children.

As a man, the potential for fatherhood is written into your body—no matter your sexual orientation, gender identity, relational status, sexual behavior, or attitude toward children. Learning to honor and appropriately express this connection between fatherhood and sexuality is central to growing into mature, responsible, non-toxic masculinity. Sex does not exist by itself and for itself. It points toward something. If you're a man, it points toward fatherhood.

We should, of course, grant that fatherhood isn't all sex is for. Sex is also for relational connection. It is for fun and recreation. Christians have also often argued that sex points to the human desire for transcendence, revealing some aspect of the mystery of God's love in the Trinity,[1] and I suspect many who reject most Christian ideas about sex would likely still agree sex is about more than just pleasure. The historic Christian perspective on sexuality has been characterized by a three-part relationship between sex, marriage, and children. Contemporary Roman Catholic thought remains most committed to these connections.[2] While I don't agree with Catholics on everything having to do with sexuality, I find the insistence on an inseparable connection between sexuality and children to be a good and body-affirming instinct.

This is not just about abortion rights, contraception, or sexual ethics, though our understanding of the purpose of sex does have significant implications for these debates. Christians should be consistent in how they speak about sex and sexuality. For men, sexuality points toward fatherhood every bit as much as it points toward motherhood for women. For men, sex is not just about having a good time and moving on with your life. This is where abortion rights activists are correct—most laws restricting abortion do little to increase male responsibility for the children they help create. Children, born and unborn, cannot be separated from the sexual choices of their fathers.

MADE TO BE FATHERS

Fatherhood is a much better prescriptive paradigm for masculinity than characteristics like leadership, dominance, difference making, and so on. Still, becoming a man isn't simply about becoming a dad. Why should it be? After all, this would exclude Jesus from the category of true manhood. So let's stop making men prove themselves by becoming married and fathering children. This is not a measure of Christian worthiness as a man; masculine identity, in Christ, goes far beyond literal fatherhood. But if male sexuality finds its proper goal in fatherhood, it means that all men are included in the paternal calling of being a male. Begetting children isn't the only way to live out a fatherly vocation in the world. Having kids makes a man a father in a literal and scientific sense, but some men who have never fathered children are far better fathers than men who have.

How should we define fatherhood then? In Genesis 1:27, we read that God created humankind "in his own image, in the image of God he created them; male and female he created them." This verse describes the creation of a sexed humanity, humanity characterized by unity and diversity, sameness and differentiation. And what comes next is of the utmost significance: "God blessed them and said to them, 'Be fruitful and increase in number; fill the earth and subdue it. Rule over the fish in the sea and the birds in the sky and over every living creature that moves on the ground'" (Gen 1:28).

These verses are often referred to as the "cultural mandate," and they have everything to do with human sexuality. Humans are blessed and told to reproduce, a central purpose of sex. But the differentiation of male and female is about more than making babies. The creation of human sexuality immediately precedes the charge to subdue, care for, and rule the world. Fatherhood is the male half of the cultural mandate.

So, how can men move through the world in a way that honors the masculine vocation of fatherhood? They can care for animals, coach a sports team, or build homes with precision and care out of concern for the people who will live in them. There are men who cultivate and plan landscaping projects, and those who are longtime employees and train new hires with care and attentiveness. Think about the man who teaches a second-grade classroom, and those who guide others on their life's journey with music. What about the man who waits tables in a restaurant, patiently attending to the dietary restrictions of his guests? Or the man who paints the church lobby? Think about the man who arranges flowers for weddings, events, and public art displays. And the man who prepares a meal in a shelter for the homeless. What about the man who taught Galilean peasants about their heavenly Father and rebuked his disciples, saying, "Let the little children come to me"?

Every one of these examples constitutes a paternal, fatherly disposition toward people, things, and creation. Not one of them requires being a literal father of children. The vocation of paternal masculinity, rightly defined, cannot and should not be reserved only for heterosexual married men. Every man is called to be a father to the world in his own way.

Neither are Christian fatherhood nor masculinity about fitting cultural masculine stereotypes. Jesus rejected many of the stereotypes of his own day. Fatherhood and maleness can look a thousand different ways, even ways that appear stereotypically feminine, a point I've tried to illustrate with the list above. Every time a man seeks to take responsibility for, cultivate, nurture, protect, repair, renew, or redeem his little corner of creation, he is acting like a father and living out the chief end of his sexuality.

WHAT FATHERHOOD TEACHES US ABOUT MALE SEXUALITY

If you're wondering what all this talk about fatherhood is doing in a book about sex, that is part of the point. We don't associate sexuality with fatherhood. That's a problem because biology makes this connection incontrovertible. The connection is not without nuance, but it is still inseparable. Looking at sexuality through the lens of fatherhood can teach us about the complexity and beauty of masculinity.

Male sexuality is relational. Fatherhood is a particular type of relationship made possible by our sexual bodies. Our bodies are intended to serve us in forming connections with other people too. Romantic relationships are not the only context in which our sexuality is relevant; they show us we are relational creatures. Through sexual embodiment we are connected to everyone who shares our bloodline—siblings, children, parents, grandparents, cousins, and beyond. Our inclination toward the beauty of other bodies and the beauty of other persons is also an aspect of our sexual existence. Because of our sexuality, we take unique delight in a conversation with another member of our own sex or a member of the opposite sex. The embodied reality of fatherhood signals that our sexual bodies are built for all manner of relationships.

Male sexuality is cooperative. Just as a man cannot become a literal father without a female body to complement his,[3] male sexuality entails a calling to cooperative, creative, and loving relationship with women in general. As Curt Thompson writes, "God has made us with desire for connection that ultimately leads to the co-creation of objects of goodness and beauty with him and others with whom we have difference, be it great or small."[4] In Genesis, Adam and Eve were created as co-regents of creation—the king and queen of God's new world. Their dominion of the earth was always intended as a cooperative affair. Men cannot do it without women. Women cannot do it without men. Any human endeavor done without the input, support, and cooperation of both sexes is not a fully human endeavor. Humanity exists, like the triune God, both in oneness and cooperation with the other. Male sexuality implies the need for and joyful participation of women in every good act of creation that humans do.

Male sexuality is life giving. Male sexuality literally creates new life. Every time a man has an orgasm, his body signals the life-giving potential of that act. Roman Catholic theologians take this to mean that every sexual act a man participates in must be open to the possibility of children. I don't go quite this far, but I see and appreciate the logical consistency of it.

The point for our purposes is that male sexuality is meant to be a life-giving force in the world. As the crisis of toxic masculinity makes clear, the aspect of maleness intended to create and nurture life has often become instead a force of destruction and death. This is a dark perversion of what our sexuality is supposed to do. Male sexuality is not only life giving, it is also self-giving. The sexual act implies a sharing of oneself for the good, flourishing, and delight of the other. Any time sex is anything other than this, it is not functioning in the way it was intended. As people of the resurrection, Christians should seek to redirect male sexuality back toward the life-giving ends for which it was created. We should be forceful and passionate enemies of all death-allied, dehumanizing expressions of male sexuality, including sexual assault, sexual abuse, coerced abortion, and sexual exploitation—especially in our church communities.

Male sexuality implies responsibility. The seriousness of sex implies a need for men to mature toward responsible, humanizing, and respectful ways of expressing their sexuality. At bare minimum this implies consent, but it goes far beyond this. Sex should entail a willingness to take on the relational implications of sharing our body with another person. At their best, Christians have sought throughout the church's history to safeguard the well-being of men, women, and children. Because of this Christians have often insisted sex be packaged with marriage, a lifelong commitment to the other's good.

The second implication of male sexual responsibility is that a man is every bit as accountable for his children as their mother is. Parents are equally expected to provide for, protect, and nurture their children. When men take care of their children, they are acting like fathers, not stepping in to fill the mother's "role." When a man changes a diaper, he does so because he loves his children, not because he's doing his wife a favor. When a man makes dinner or cleans the dishes, he is living into the responsible expression of his sexuality, not helping his wife with the housework. Together and in equal partnership with their mother, a father is responsible for the entirety of his children's well-being, not just their financial needs or physical safety.

Male sexuality is nurturing. The idea that men aren't, can't, or shouldn't be nurturing is toxic. In the Gospels, Jesus shares many tender moments with his disciples and followers. The paternal, nurturing urge is present in many of the godly men I know. I've seen it in good pastors, youth volunteers, nursery workers, friends, my own father, and my brothers and brothers-in-law. It is apparent in the way good men relate to the vulnerable and young people around them. It shouldn't be a big deal, much less something we intentionally disassociate from masculinity.

The nurturing ends of masculine sexuality have implications for men's other relationships. Men should, when relevant, take their physical advantage into account. They should consider their strength and privilege in all their relationships. They should leverage their embodied male advantage for the well-being of others, not preservation of power or self-seeking ends.

Male sexuality is self-sacrificial. Kids are inconvenient. My responsibility to my children regularly distracts me from other things I'd like to be doing. These interruptions have, for instance, made it much more difficult to write this book. But the meaning my children bring to my life is not worth comparing with these relatively minor inconveniences. Being a father and husband is a joy and a privilege, but it involves significant sacrifices. In the church we often romanticize married life. My life as a married man has many benefits, but it also limits my freedom and opportunities. As Jonathan Grant writes, "Marriage is a gift, but it's also a crisis."[5] There's something redemptive about the inconvenience of children. It reminds us that we cannot live out our sexuality independent of love and sacrifice. Healthy expressions of male sexuality embrace this reality; toxic expressions of male sexuality deny it or avoid it.

WITH GREAT POWER COMES GREAT RESPONSIBILITY

Christian books, resources, and teaching on sex too often say almost nothing about fatherhood. This absence is not only a disservice to families and children, it is an incomplete understanding of male sexuality. Men and boys must learn to see their sexuality in terms of the calling of fatherhood.

Sex is not merely about pleasure or self-fulfillment. Pleasure should lead to deeper connection in relationships. Relationships lead to new life, opportunities, limitations, and responsibility. Too often in Christian contexts (and society in general), women carry an unfair share of the responsibility associated with human sexuality. This should not be so. Sex is a powerful thing, and with great power comes great responsibility. If you're a man, God made you sexual to show you that growing up means becoming a father.

FIFTEEN

DEATH AND RESURRECTION
THE BEAUTY OF REDEEMED MASCULINITY

SEXUAL SATISFACTION IS ELUSIVE. Life circumstances, fractured relationships, sinful mistakes, non-sinful mistakes, physical con-
dition, low self-confidence, anxiety, and abuse all make finding the
"right person" and enjoying sex with them difficult and complicated.
Few cultures throughout history have totalized the significance of
sex more than the modern West. Our sexuality and the way we
express it is, for many, the essence of who we are.

The call of the Christian life does not mean renouncing all
sexual activity. However, at the very least, the Christian call
means renouncing a claim to sex on our own terms. Sexuality
should not be just about me and what I want. It is a part of
our humanity intended to bring life and bless others. Despite
patriarchal and dehumanizing expressions of the faith, Christians have been agents and advocates of rehumanization
throughout the church's two-thousand-year history.[1] In her best
expressions, the church brings life, not death. The toxic masculinity that has infected the church is a parasite on the Christian
vision of sex and sexuality. Dehumanization is not Christian.
Rehumanization is.

184 PART III: GROWING UP, BECOMING A MAN

CULTURAL AND CHRISTIAN IDOLS OF SEXUAL FULFILLMENT

Conservative Christians are known for their vocal opposition to the LGBTQ+ movement and sexual liberation. Part of this opposition includes a critique of the culture's idols of sexual fulfillment and self-determination. In considering this common critique, I'm reminded of the words of Jesus:

> Do not judge, or you too will be judged. For in the same way you judge others, you will be judged, and with the measure you use, it will be measured to you. Why do you look at the speck of sawdust in your brother's eye and pay no attention to the plank in your own eye? How can you say to your brother, "Let me take the speck out of your eye," when all the time there is a plank in your own eye? You hypocrite, first take the plank out of your own eye, and then you will see clearly to remove the speck from your brother's eye. (Matt 7:1-5)

At the risk of being too on the nose, allow me to paraphrase: *Christians, be careful how you judge the culture's sexual immorality. For God will hold you to the same standard you use to oppress, harm, and exclude others. Why are you so concerned about what others think and do with their sexuality when you offer safe haven to abusers in your churches? How dare you presume to rebuke the culture's idolatry of sex! First, worry about yourselves. Get your own house in order, then you might actually be in a position to say something helpful to the culture.*

Purity culture shows that Christians are not innocent of fashioning idols designed to guarantee sexual fulfillment—particularly for men. We have twisted biblical passages, preserved male power and privilege, and harmed women and children inside and outside the community of faith. We have obsessed over the speck in the culture's eye while neglecting the log in our own. Sex is the ground on which many of our culture wars and identity politics are fought. Because we have idolized sex, sex has become holy ground.

Because we have made sex our god, we respond with ferocity when someone threatens our access to it. Christians are often just as guilty of this as non-Christians.

But having great sex isn't what Christianity is about. If you stick with Jesus because you think following biblical rules will lead to your best sex life, I have bad news for you: God has promised you no such thing. The Christian life is one of self-denial, not self-fulfillment. To move beyond our subcultural sickness, Christian men need to embrace giving up their sense of entitlement to sexual satisfaction, single or married.

Few people would willingly give up their chance at having a great sex life. We understand the value of sexual fulfillment. Still, God calls us to be willing to give up things that are precious to us. Like any good father, he loves giving us good gifts, but he loves us more than he loves giving us gifts. In a broken world, we often become preoccupied with the gifts at the expense of our humanity and the humanity of others. When this happens, it is God's kindness that he calls us to let go of what we hold most dear. Maybe, like Job, after a season of suffering, we will receive back what we have lost. But maybe not. Maybe God wants to, instead, give us the gift of himself. As C. S. Lewis writes in the preface to *The Great Divorce*, "I believe, to be sure, that any man who reaches Heaven will find that what he abandoned (even in plucking out his right eye) has not been lost: that the kernel of what he was really seeking even in his most depraved wishes will be there, beyond expectation, waiting for him in 'the High Countries.'"[2]

SEX-POSITIVE, BODY-POSITIVE CHRISTIANITY

Some have suggested body positivity and sex positivity as the solution to purity culture.[3] I believe Christianity is both radically body positive and profoundly sex positive. But the Christian versions of body and sex positivity are different from the culture at large. Christianity is not anti-sex—there's a whole book in the Bible about it. It's also not anti-body. The man Christians claim as Savior died and rose to save our broken bodies, and as Paul writes in Romans 8, we eagerly await their redemption. God made our bodies and loves them so much that he saved them from corruption and death.

Christianity has been part of too many body-shaming, misogynistic, sex-skeptical movements throughout its history. But I believe these are not representative of true Christian faith. The strict application of culturally situated sexual roles is not Christianity. Likewise, the prudish suppression of sexuality and hatred of sexual bodies is not Christianity. But neither is Jesus the champion of sexual liberation some claim he is. As with all things, Jesus does not fit into the box conservatives or progressives put him in to suit their ideological agendas. Jesus is too busy being Lord of the universe to be co-opted for someone's culture war.

At the beginning of this book, I talked about several groups I had in mind as I wrote. One was those of you who have been so harmed, disappointed, or disgusted by the church that you feel you can't even be part of it anymore. I want you to know I still see you. I don't envision what I've written here as the cure-all for your doubts and misgivings. However, I believe Jesus, together with his Father, is your ally, not your enemy. He stands on your side against oppression and dehumanization—even when those who sin against you claim to represent him. God's judgment is not idle, and he will set to right what has been wronged.

I'm also mindful of LGBTQ+ Christians, allies, and activists. Maybe you wish I had said things differently. That's understandable. I hope you can see how I've tried to include your experiences and perspectives within this conversation. My Christian tradition, like all traditions, has its boundaries. I've tried to stay within those boundaries, but my boundaries may not be yours—I respect and understand that. I don't expect you to agree with everything I've said in this book, but I've done my best to present a life-giving vision of masculinity that can serve all men, regardless of their sexual orientation or erotic inclinations.

DEATH IS THE PATH TO LIFE

Sex, like all areas of growth in godliness, is about giving yourself up. It took me a long time to learn this—I'm still learning it. I've caused pain to myself, the women I've been in relationships with, and my wife through my stubborn and dehumanizing attitudes and actions. Unlearning this has been a type of death. It included the death of dreams for my honeymoon, marriage, and our youngest years together. My story is just one example (and perhaps not an especially difficult one) of the types of pain some people experience in connection with sex.

Here's something I've thought a lot about in recent years: What if God gave me my sexuality to teach me self-denial? This isn't purity culture's self-denial for delayed gratification. This is the self-denial of giving up something I was taught to expect, something I badly desired. But I'm choosing to trust that life will come from this small death. And I trust God more than I trust myself. He is committed to my good, and he is forming me into a more whole version of myself.

Growing up into a mature, non-toxic masculine sexuality will mean continuing to learn that the richest things in life are not about self-gratification, but self-surrender and self-giving. Continued growth in Christian virtue is not about "staying pure." There is only one who is pure, and he himself is our purity. Progress in faithful expressions of sexuality means growing up, becoming more human, and cultivating the virtue of chastity, single or married. As we die to our sinful, dehumanizing nature, we will finally be set free, bit by bit, from the clutches of death. As with all Christian stories, death is not the end. We must die to be made alive (John 12:24).

It really is a beautiful thing to be a man. Yes, the culture and even the church have corrupted the goodness of masculinity, but in

Christ, it need not be so. Men, the path forward for you is to affirm the created goodness of your maleness. Men can be good and beautiful human beings, not in spite of their maleness or sexual desire, but because of it.

People need to see the Christian vision for sex as beautiful if it is going to sustain them through the sexual suffering they may find in various points in their life. I understand it's relatively easy for me, as a cisgendered, heterosexual male, to claim that sex ought to be reserved for a relationship between one man and one woman within the covenant of marriage. I get that it may sound ridiculously old-fashioned, even toxic, to some of you.

Despite all this, I believe that living according to the traditional Christian sexual ethic is good. Anyone who sets out to write a book critiquing purity culture will inevitably face the question, "Well, what are you going to teach your kids about premarital sex?" I'll commend the Christian sexual ethic to my children—yes, including encouraging them to wait until marriage—because I still believe it's a beautiful way to live. It's a way of living that honors the goodness of sex, bodies, children, and marriage. It honors the witness of Scripture and the best aspects of the Christian tradition. I also believe that—when separated from the dehumanizing elements of evangelicalism's purity culture and wider society's promiscuity culture—Christian sexual ethics promote human flourishing.

Finally, I believe living according to the traditional Christian sexual ethic is good *for me*. Painful, sometimes lonely, often frustrating—but good. Leaning into a more permissive sexual ethic would have been destructive for me, for Shelby, and for our kids. If our marriage were to fall apart, our children would suffer most. If the biblical teaching is that sex, marriage, and children go together, then my adherence to that ethic means a loving and stable life for my kids. I will, without hesitation, give up my sexual fulfillment for their sake.

Shelby and I have walked a difficult road together for these eight years of marriage. When we let it, the pain of our sexual struggles serves to draw us together, not push us apart. We haven't had the mind-blowing sex my adolescent self might have hoped for. But even our imperfect sex life is *ours*. The moments we do share together are meaningful because they're hard fought through sorrow, disappointment, fear, and shame. And the difficulty we face in this regard makes our relationship that much more beautiful.

The traditional Christian sexual ethic has given me all this. Yes, it has also been a source of pain. Despite this, I have found God to be good. I remain a Christian, not because the sex is worth it, but because Jesus is worth it.

Living into non-toxic masculinity is not a matter of following rules for maintaining sexual purity and avoiding sexual sin. It's about growing up. The path to wholeness is often complicated, and it may involve steps forward and steps back. Purity is something we mature into. It's a difficult process, and the journey may feel like it's going kill us. But with God, death is the path to life. But even this death is not a repudiation of our sexual selves or destruction of our desire. Curt Thompson writes, "For the world to be redeemed, God does not destroy desire; rather, he resurrects and renews it while using it to renew everything else, beginning with us."[4]

So what is non-toxic masculinity? It is rehumanized masculinity, conformed to the image of the true man, Jesus of Nazareth. In Christ, we are raised to newness of life, seated with him in the heavenly places. We have already been made new, but we are not yet fully who we will be. Non-toxic masculinity grows up into the holy and virtuous selves we are destined to be. It embraces the virtue of chastity, "which sees others as belonging to God and not as a means of self-fulfillment."[5] Faithful, non-toxic masculinity imitates Christ, giving up ourselves to serve others. Throughout this process, we are transformed by the renewing of our minds, growing toward a redeemed sexuality characterized by love, joy, peace, patience, kindness, goodness, faithfulness, gentleness, and self-control. If that's not a good definition of what non-toxic sexuality should look like, I don't know what is.

TREVOR'S STORY

Like me, Trevor was homeschooled for much of his childhood. His parents were in ministry, and the Bible was a central part of his upbringing. He also described himself as a sensitive and romantic person.

He told me, "I have a clear memory of sitting and gaping at the girls running around in AWANA. Not in a sexual way—I couldn't have been more than seven or eight. Just like, *Wow, they're so beautiful.*"

When Trevor was eleven years old his mom caught him kissing a girl in the neighborhood. "I got reprimanded, and there are two things I remember from that conversation. One was that the Bible was used as ammo to show me why everything I was doing was wrong. The second was that my mom told me I had stolen from my dad the ability to say on my wedding day that that was my first kiss."

This was the first time Trevor had ever heard of such an expectation, and in the same moment he found out about it, he found out he had fallen short. The sex education Trevor got from his parents turned out to be too little too late. "Sex wasn't talked about much until I had already seen pornography and was already crushing on every girl I saw." As he got older, he learned more about his parents' expectations for his purity. "I remember feeling like it had already been botched, like I had ruined something. I figured I might as well just keep doing what I was doing. There's nothing left to persevere for."

He continued to pine after girls. Trevor told me, "From as early as I can remember, I wanted girls to want me." Trevor's family moved to a new state while he was in high school. As he got plugged in at his new Christian school, a couple of the boys in the community played a cruel prank on him. They got Trevor's phone number and texted him pretending to be one of the girls in the group they suspected Trevor was interested in. They coaxed the conversation in a sexual direction to bait Trevor into saying something embarrassing. Trevor went along with it and was humiliated when the boys publicly shared these sexual and flirtatious texts.

This embarrassment added another layer of shame to Trevor's already tortured adolescent sexuality. "For me, saying no to drugs was easy. But sex was the worst thing you could ever do, and it's something I always had a hard time with." The experience with the boys at school rocked Trevor with "shame to the core." He spiraled into a depression from which he didn't recover for years.

He indulged more and more in his sexual desires. In college, he became "incredibly efficient" at seeking out sex if he wanted it. His emotional wounds festered. "One thing that kept me seeking sex was my inability to process emotions in a healthy way."

He had abandoned creative outlets he enjoyed because they didn't fit the masculine mold he was given at church. "We were told women are emotional, and I thought, *Why am I emotional, then?* For guys, emotions were bad things, and when you experience them, you need to push them down." All the while, Trevor continued to struggle with controlling his sexual behavior. Purity culture didn't have an answer for people like him who had already botched their purity. "The solution is to get more accountability, but for someone like me, that just added another layer of shame." On their own, added layers of accountability or Scripture memory offered little help.

At this point Trevor was "having sex like crazy. Women became a type of healing for me. All the romantic aspects of sex were gone, it was just a way to feel good so I didn't have to feel lonely or sad or depressed." In his early twenties, Trevor was desperate. His desperation led him to keep pursuing sex in more risky ways. Around this time, Trevor moved again. As he plugged into a new community, someone gave him a copy of *Every Man's Battle*. But rather than double down on purity culture's approach, Trevor began pursuing friendships. "Purity culture was not helpful at that time. But I found discipleship helpful. Discipleship made me feel loved—and liked."

Trevor paused pensively as he told me his story. Then he continued, as if he had realized something just in that moment, "Purity culture doesn't like you."

I was struck at this statement. *Purity culture doesn't like you.* Yes, purity was motivated by a genuine concern, even love for young people, but does anyone feel liked by purity culture's pronouncement about the dangers of premarital sex or the inevitability of men and boys' sexual struggles? Men don't need to be told over and over that their natural sexual inclinations are despicable and dangerous. They need to feel loved, accepted, and delighted in. They need to feel liked.

Trevor pursued more meaningful friendships and relationships with mentors. He began to see a Christian therapist. He started to disentangle his sense of self from the shame that accompanied his sexual choices. "I placed my identity in the things I did. I knew I was saved, but I still felt like the things I did affected the way God viewed me. It wasn't until much later, through some good friends and a Christian therapist, that I realized that God, when he looks at me, sees me through the lens of Jesus. That he's pleased. And he likes what he sees."

Trevor reengaged his creative side and began to process his wounds through poetry and spoken-word. Most importantly, he began to believe that God delights in him. He saw his journey as growth toward wholeness, not through a paradigm of purity that was already lost and could never be regained.

Trevor told me that he is still in process, but it's a process characterized by joy. He told me, "I will be my pure self in Christ, whole, complete, lacking in nothing, in the year 3021. But I can also experience that wholeness now. I can experience the kingdom of heaven now. I can learn to process my emotions and my insecurities to give myself more of my future self, my free self."

WHERE DO WE GO FROM HERE?

Pastors, parents, married, single, men, women, gay, straight—we all have a role to play in the reformation of the church into a more humanizing place. One call of the Protestant Reformation was *semper reformanda*, the conviction that the church should be always reforming. I believe we are in a season of reform in our attitudes and behaviors surrounding sexuality, particularly in how we dehumanize women. This is important work we all must be committed to. If we seek God and humbly repent, he can bring life out of death.

God calls us to life that is truly life. The idols of sexual fulfillment are false gods. These idols have dehumanized many of us, even as they promised life. The wise father warns of the adulterous woman: "Her feet go down to death; her steps lead straight to the grave" (Prov 5:5).

But even if we have followed the gods of sex to the grave, there is one who speaks life even to dead men—the one who spoke to his friend in Galilee two thousand years ago:

"Lazarus, come out."

Christ has died, taking upon himself the brokenness of our fractured humanity, including the crushing loneliness we experience in sexual suffering.

Christ is risen, demonstrating the path of life through death, that self-sacrifice and self-denial culminate in a renewal of our bodies and our sexual nature.

ACKNOWLEDGMENTS

THIS WAS A DIFFICULT BOOK TO WRITE. I'm sure that's the case for most first-time authors, but its personal nature and controversial subject matter made for an emotionally and spiritually tumultuous writing and editing process. Looking back, I'm mindful of the many people who encouraged, supported, and challenged me along the way.

First, thank you to the editorial team at InterVarsity Press, who expressed enthusiasm for the project from the start. I'm especially grateful to Ethan McCarthy for his careful, wise, and challenging feedback. I'm thankful also to Tianna Haas for her insight and suggestions during the editing process.

I also want to acknowledge my dear friends and colleagues at the Center for Pastor Theologians: Todd Wilson, Joel Lawrence, and Rae Paul, who all put up with my regular updates and questions about the project and served as a sounding board during the process. Todd was instrumental in the very early stages, encouraging me not to quickly dismiss the idea of writing this book, even though I had just recently embarked on a PhD program. It felt foolhardy at the time—indeed, it was foolhardy—but Todd encouraged me to listen to the stirring in my heart as I emotionally processed the news of the Atlanta spa shootings in March 2021.

Likewise, I want to thank my friends and coursemates at the University of Oxford, many of whom encouraged me at various points in writing and editing. I'm especially grateful to David Williams, who listened to me agonize and offered advice about this project on several occasions over a pint at the pub.

To the Randolph Crew, Joy Martin-Sinclair and Janae Horst: your enthusiastic support of this book from day one has meant more to me than you know. You are both very dear to me, and I am privileged to count you as sisters and friends. Thank you for sharing your lives with me and allowing me to share mine with you.

Several other friends provided encouraging conversations and emails at key points in the process, including generous offers to review portions of the manuscript. Thank you, Gerald Hiestand, Amy Peeler, Wes Hill, Mike Bailey, and Andrew and Jamie Peterson.

A most sincere thank you is in order to each of the men and women who agreed to let me interview them for this project. Your vulnerability, courage, faith, and resilience are a genuine inspiration to me. Thank you for trusting me with your stories.

Finally, to my love, Shelby Deann. As trite as it is to say, I could not have done this without you—and you know that. Whatever courage I have is thanks to you. I will forever cherish the hours spent poring over the manuscript and reading chapter drafts together. This book is every bit as much yours as it is mine. Thank you for allowing me to share our story. As difficult as it's been, I wouldn't change a thing. For your love, faithfulness, and loyalty—I am blessed beyond measure. Thank you for being my safe place.

NOTES

INTRODUCTION: WAKE UP, GUYS

[1] Chanel Miller, *Know My Name: The Survivor of the Stanford Sexual Assault Case Tells Her Story* (London: Penguin Books, 2020), 357.

[2] This sense of sexual entitlement, taken to its logical extreme, has given rise to the so-called incel community. Short for "involuntary celibate," incels are an online group of men who struggle to find sexual partners and thus believe they are being treated unfairly by women. Perhaps unsurprisingly, this attitude sometimes ends in violence, as was the case in 2014 when self-identified incel Elliot Rodger went on a killing spree in southern California. For a feminist examination and critique of this event, the incel movement, and sexual entitlement, see Amia Srinivasan, *The Right to Sex* (London: Bloomsbury, 2021), 73-91.

[3] Jackson Katz, *The Macho Paradox: Why Some Men Hurt Women and How All Men Can Help* (Naperville, IL: Source Books, 2019), 17.

[4] The final phrase is my own translation of the Greek, intended to draw out the clear contrast Paul is making in the passage between the Christian community and wider world.

[5] Samuel L. Perry, "Not Practicing What You Preach: Religion and Incongruence Between Pornography Beliefs and Usage," *The Journal of Sex Research* 55, no. 3 (2018): 369-80, https://doi.org/10.1080/00224499.2017.1333569.

[6] One survey found that 12 percent of married Christian women never or almost never have an orgasm during sex. Eleven percent orgasm less than half of the time they have sex. See Sheila Wray Gregoire, Rebecca Gregoire Lindenbach, and Joanna Sawatsky, *The Great Sex Rescue: The Lies You've Been Taught and How to Recover What God Intended* (Grand Rapids, MI: Baker, 2021), 41.

[7] Lyman Stone and W. Bradford Wilcox, "The Religious Marriage Paradox: Younger Marriage, Less Divorce," *Institute for Family Studies* blog, December 15, 2021, https://ifstudies.org/blog/the-religious-marriage-paradox-younger-marriage-less-divorce.

[8] The one exception I have found is Matthias Roberts's LGBTQ+ perspective in *Beyond Shame: Creating a Healthy Sex Life on Your Own Terms* (Minneapolis: Fortress Press, 2020).

[9]See Rachael Denhollander, *What Is a Girl Worth? My Story of Breaking the Silence and Exposing the Truth about Larry Nassar and USA Gymnastics* (Carol Stream, IL: Tyndale, 2019).

[10]Rachael Denhollander, "I don't even know where to begin," Facebook, May 7, 2021, www.facebook.com/OfficialDenhollander/posts/pfbid0LGSXb4fEHS NG7iqEV84wM8DGCZ3jbwtUQgHTcn2jP8D3uDesktnKdEgaY4l8h7wBl.

1. WHAT IS "PURITY CULTURE"?

[1]See especially Rachel Joy Welcher, *Talking Back to Purity Culture: Rediscovering Faithful Christian Sexuality* (Downers Grove, IL: InterVarsity Press, 2019); and Sheila Wray Gregoire, Rebecca Gregoire Lindenbach, and Joanna Sawatsky's *The Great Sex Rescue: The Lies You've Been Taught and How to Recover What God Intended* (Grand Rapids, MI: Baker, 2021).

[2]Sara Moslener makes a similar point in *Virgin Nation: Sexual Purity and American Adolescence* (New York: Oxford University Press, 2015), 124.

[3]At the peak of the baby boom in 1959, the birth rate was almost triple what it had been in 1940. For an overview of the historical factors accounting for this rise in births and focus on family life, see Doug Owram, *Born at the Right Time: A History of the Baby Boom Generation* (Toronto: University of Toronto Press, 1996), 1-30.

[4]Owram, *Born at the Right Time*, 6.

[5]For a conservative account and critique of the sexual revolution and the philosophical and cultural forces that gave rise to it, see Carl R. Trueman, *The Rise and Triumph of the Modern Self: Cultural Amnesia, Expressive Individualism, and the Road to Sexual Revolution* (Wheaton, IL: Crossway, 2020). My assessment of Trueman's account is mixed, but I won't go into the details here.

[6]Andrew L. Whitehead and Samuel L. Perry, *Taking America Back for God: Christian Nationalism in the United States* (New York: Oxford University Press, 2020), 125-27.

[7]For the sake of illustration, see Kristin Kobes Du Mez's account of the work of James Dobson and Tim LaHaye during this time in *Jesus and John Wayne: How White Evangelicals Corrupted a Faith and Fractured a Nation* (New York: Liveright, 2020), 78-87, 89-95.

[8]Whitehead and Perry, *Taking America Back for God*, 121-49.

[9]Moslener, *Virgin Nation*, 110.

[10]See Jean M. Twenge, Ryne A. Sherman, and Brooke E. Wells, "Declines in Sexual Frequency Among American Adults, 1989–2014," *Archives of Sexual Behavior* 46, no. 8 (2017): 2389-401; and Scott J. South and Lei Lei, "Why Are Fewer Young Adults Having Casual Sex?" *Socius* 7, no. 1 (January 2021).

[11]John Elflein, "Antidepressant Use Among Teenagers in the U.S. from 2015–2019, by Gender," *Statista*, July 17, 2020, www.statista.com/statistics/1133612/anti depressant-use-teenagers-by-gender-us/.

[12]Christine Leong et al., "Psychotropic Drug Use in Children and Adolescents Before and During the COVID-19 Pandemic," *JAMA Pediatrics* 176, no. 3 (January 4, 2022): 318-20.

[13]See, for example, Rebecca Jennings's interview with Nancy Jo Sales, "Why Dating Apps Make You Feel Awful," *Vox*, May 19, 2021, www.vox.com/the-goods /22442114/nancy-jo-sales-nothing-personal-tinder-bumble-hinge-dating-apps.

[14]A report published by Barna in October 2021 (*Millennials in America*) found that 39 percent of Americans aged 18–24 identify as LGBTQ+.

[15]For more thorough and technical historical treatments, see Du Mez's *Jesus and John Wayne*; Christine Gardner's *Making Chastity Sexy* (Berkeley: University of California Press, 2015); Moslener's *Virgin Nation*; Mark Regnerus's *Forbidden Fruit* (New York: Oxford University Press, 2007); and *Premarital Sex in America* (New York: Oxford University Press, 2010), which Regnerus coauthored with Jeremy Eucker.

2. THE "GREAT SEX" PROSPERITY GOSPEL

[1]James B. Nelson, *Embodiment: An Approach to Sexuality and Christian Theology* (Minneapolis: Augsburg, 1978), 78-79.

[2]Emily Joy Allison makes a similar point while discussing the policing of women's clothing that remains common in churches and youth groups in #*ChurchToo: How Purity Culture Upholds Abuse and How to Find Healing* (Minneapolis: Broadleaf Books, 2021), 50.

[3]C. S. Lewis imagines a demon's disdain for the humans because they are a "revolting hybrid" of spiritual and physical, *The Screwtape Letters* (New York: HarperCollins, 2012), 37.

[4]Katelyn Beaty, "Joshua Harris and the Sexual Prosperity Gospel," *Religion News Service*, July 26, 2019, https://religionnews.com/2019/07/26/joshua-harris-and -the-sexual-prosperity-gospel.

[5]Christine Gardner, *Making Chastity Sexy: The Rhetoric of Evangelical Abstinence Campaigns* (Berkeley: University of California Press, 2011), 51. Gardner describes in detail the shameless strategies used to promote premarital abstinence, including a T-shirt emblazoned with "How to Have the Best Sex Ever" distributed at a youth purity rally.

[6]Amia Srinivasan, *The Right to Sex* (London: Bloomsbury, 2021), 82. Srinivasan goes on to partially critique this perspective, noting feminism's understandable

but not unproblematic "reluctance to interrogate the formation of our desires" (p. 83). She goes on, "The sex-positive gaze risks covering not only for misogyny, but for racism, ableism, transphobia and every other oppressive system that makes its way into the bedroom through the seemingly innocuous mechanism of 'personal preference'" (p. 84).

[7]Samuel L. Perry, *Addicted to Lust: Pornography in the Lives of Conservative Protestants* (New York: Oxford University Press, 2019), 179.

[8]Christine Emba, *Rethinking Sex: A Provocation* (New York: Sentinel, 2022), 99.

[9]Bridget Eileen Rivera, *Heavy Burdens: Seven Ways LGBTQ Christians Experience Harm in the Church* (Grand Rapids, MI: Brazos, 2021), 33-39.

[10]Rivera, *Heavy Burdens*, 38-39.

[11]Jonathan Grant makes a similar point describing the modern West's "culture of authenticity." While his critique falls harder on the culture than the church, he grants that Christians can adopt their own version of "Soul Mate Salvation." *Divine Sex: A Compelling Vision for Christian Relationships in a Hypersexualized Age* (Grand Rapids, MI: Brazos, 2015), 47-48.

3. THE DEHUMANIZATION OF MEN

[1]For instance, the sexual rights of powerful men were assumed in Ancient Roman society. It was the emergence of Christianity and the teaching of such early Christians like the Apostle Paul that began to seriously challenge the routine victimization of women and boys by these men. See Tom Holland, *Dominion: The Making of the Western Mind* (London: Little, Brown, 2019), 81.

[2]As it relates to power imbalances in sexual encounters, Christine Emba describes this dynamic in stark, even uncomfortable terms: "The majority of men could likely kill a woman with their bare hands. Hence the mental calculus that women face whenever they want to reject a man's sexual advances: Will he hurt me?" *Rethinking Sex: A Provocation* (New York: Sentinel, 2022), 70.

[3]*Oxford Dictionary Online*, s.v. "toxic masculinity," accessed August 29, 2022, https://premium.oxforddictionaries.com/definition/english/toxic-masculinity?q=toxic+masculinity.

[4]More recently, as this male gaze has been critiqued, designers and directors have slowly started to make changes. For example, a recent rerelease of the popular videogame series *Mass Effect* edited the way a female character was portrayed in the original release. The original 2010 version of the game included obvious examples of this male gaze design: several awkwardly low and extended camera angles that fixated on this female character's butt. The 2021 rerelease edited these angles to more natural, eye-level portrayals.

[5]Stephen Arterburn and Fred Stoeker, *Every Man's Battle: Winning the War on Sexual Temptation One Victory at a Time* (Colorado Springs: WaterBrook, 2009), 61. See also the excellent discussion of this and similar purity culture quotes in Sheila Wray Gregoire, Rebecca Gregoire Lindenbach, and Joanna Sawatsky's *The Great Sex Rescue: The Lies You've Been Taught and How to Recover What God Intended* (Grand Rapids, MI: Baker, 2021), 78.

[6]The claim that men are more easily visually stimulated than women has questionable scientific support. For an accessible discussion see Sheila Gregoire, "Are 'Pink Brains' and 'Blue Brains' Real?" September 30, 2021, in *Bare Marriage*, podcast, https://podcasts.apple.com/us/podcast/episode-115-are-pink-brains -and-blue-brains-real/id1448888894?i=1000537099230.

[7]Christian leaders, however, are often given passes on even these sins. For an excellent discussion of this alarming pattern, see Diane Langberg's *Redeeming Power: Understanding Authority and Abuse in the Church* (Grand Rapids, MI: Brazos, 2020).

[8]Feminist critique of consent-only sexual ethics have become more common in recent years. For instance, Amia Srinivasan writes, "When we see consent as the sole constraint on ethically OK sex, we are pushed towards a naturalisation of sexual preference in which the rape fantasy becomes a primordial rather than a political fact," in *The Right to Sex: Feminism in the Twenty-First Century* (New York: Farrar, Straus and Giroux, 2021), 84. The implication here is that if such a fantasy is a fact of nature, it becomes more difficult to critique on moral grounds. This approach, she argues, gives cover to all manner of sexual violence and discrimination baked into patriarchal social and political systems. The question of how consent-only sexual ethics fall short is also the topic of Christine Emba's thought-provoking book, *Rethinking Sex*.

[9]Curt Thompson, *The Soul of Desire: Discovering the Neuroscience of Longing, Beauty, and Community* (Downers Grove, IL: InterVarsity Press, 2021), 17.

[10]Thompson, *Soul of Desire*, 22.

[11]See especially Mike Cosper, "The Things We Do to Women," July 26, 2021, in *The Rise and Fall of Mars Hill*, podcast, www.christianitytoday.com/ct/podcasts/rise -and-fall-of-mars-hill/mars-hill-mark-driscoll-podcast-things-we-do-women .html.

[12]Jeanine Santucci, Jim Sergent, and George Petras, "19 Women Have Accused Trump of Sexual Misconduct. Here's What Their Stories Have in Common," *USA Today*, October 21, 2020, www.usatoday.com/in-depth/news/investigations /2020/10/21/trump-sexual-assault-allegations-share-similar-patterns-19-women /5279155002.

[13]Nate Pyle, *Man Enough: How Jesus Redefines Manhood* (Grand Rapids, MI: Zondervan, 2015), 19.

[14]Nate Pyle makes a similar point in *Man Enough*, 35.

4. THE DEHUMANIZATION OF WOMEN

[1]Emily Joy Allison, *#ChurchToo: How Purity Culture Upholds Abuse and How to Find Healing* (Minneapolis: Broadleaf Books, 2021), 105.

[2]Allison, *#ChurchToo*, 1-19.

[3]On this point see Bridget Eileen Rivera, *Heavy Burdens: Seven Ways LGBTQ Christians Experience Harm in the Church* (Grand Rapids, MI: Brazos, 2021), 183-90.

[4]Allison, *#ChurchToo*, 105.

[5]Rachel Joy Welcher, *Talking Back to Purity Culture: Rediscovering Faithful Christian Sexuality* (Downers Grove, IL: InterVarsity Press, 2019), 52-53.

[6]Welcher, *Talking Back to Purity Culture*, 113.

[7]Welcher, *Talking Back to Purity Culture*, 117.

[8]Linda Kay Klein, *Pure: Inside the Evangelical Movement That Shamed a Generation of Women and How I Broke Free* (New York: Atria, 2022), 139.

[9]Not everyone has moved on, though. In 2022, conservative theologian Owen Strachan devoted a one-hour podcast episode to the topic. Strachan's answer, in short: absolutely not. Owen Strachan, "Should Women Wear Tight Leggings? A Biblical Approach to the Beauty of Modesty," April 22, 2022, in *The Antithesis*, podcast, https://podcasts.apple.com/us/podcast/should-women-wear-tight-leggings-a-biblical/id1152518569?i=1000558336598.

[10]Welcher, *Talking Back to Purity Culture*, 32.

5. VICTIMS OF OUR OWN DESIRE?

[1]Linda Kay Klein describes this dynamic memorably in *Pure: Inside the Evangelical Movement That Shamed a Generation of Women and How I Broke Free* (New York: Atria, 2022), 4.

[2]Of course, many girls and women often experienced this second type of shame as well.

[3]Charles Marsh, *Evangelical Anxiety: A Memoir* (San Francisco: HarperOne, 2022), 155.

[4]Curt Thompson, *The Soul of Shame: Retelling the Stories We Believe About Ourselves* (Downers Grove, IL: InterVarsity Press, 2015), 63.

[5]Thompson, *Soul of Shame*, 31.

[6]Thompson, *Soul of Shame*, 31.

[7]Jay Stringer, *Unwanted: How Sexual Brokenness Reveals Our Way to Healing* (Colorado Springs: NavPress, 2018), 6.

[8]I am indebted to an email exchange with my friend Joseph L. for many of the ideas and illustrations contained in this section.

[9]I'm happy to report that in the time between writing and publication, Grace has repented of her insect-murdering ways.

[10]Larry Crabb, *Men of Courage: God's Call to Move Beyond the Silence of Adam* (Grand Rapids, MI: Zondervan, 2013), 58-67.

[11]Stringer, *Unwanted*, 60.

[12]Stringer, *Unwanted*, 38.

6. THE BIBLE SAYS SO

[1]Jonathan Grant, *Divine Sex: A Compelling Vision for Christian Relationships in a Hypersexualized Age* (Grand Rapids, MI: Brazos, 2015), 34.

[2]This teaching is often closely associated with the popular books by Shaunti Feldhahn, *For Women Only* and *For Men Only*. See especially *For Women Only: What You Need to Know About the Inner Lives of Men* (Colorado Springs: Multnomah, 2004), 91-136.

[3]Terri D. Fischer, Zachary T. Moore, and Mary-Jo Pittenger, "Sex on the Brain? An Examination of Frequency of Sexual Cognitions as a Function of Gender, Erotophilia, and Social Desirability," *The Journal of Sex Research* 49, no. 1 (2012): 69-77.

[4]An important side note: Victims of sexual abuse and assault are often deeply affected in their experience of sexual desire. For many, this plays a larger role in their libido than their gender.

[5]Similar problems of male-centric translations are characteristic of the ESV. For a historical account of the gender bias in English Bible translation, see Beth Allison Barr, *The Making of Biblical Womanhood: How the Subjugation of Women Became Gospel Truth* (Grand Rapids, MI: Brazos, 2021), 129-50. See also, Samuel Perry, "The Bible as a Product of Cultural Power: The Case of Gender Ideology in the English Standard Version." *Sociology of Religion* 81(1):68-92.

7. THE TRUE MAN

[1]From the Greek *dokeō*, "to seem, appear."

[2]You can read a published version of my pastor's sermon in Todd Wilson, *Mere Sexuality: Rediscovering the Christian Vision of Sexuality* (Grand Rapids, MI: Zondervan, 2016).

[3]Does Jesus' maleness exclude women? Or does it imply that men are more important or holy than women? These are important questions, and I believe the answer to both is no. The incarnation of God through a woman constitutes a radical reaffirmation of the goodness of female bodies. As Amy Peeler writes, "That God was born of a woman—the mode of the incarnation—determines

how all Christians view the triune God as well as all people made in the divine image. Consequently, if the Christian God does not value women, the entire system crumbles, and we Christians are, of all people, most to be pitied. Blessedly, it is the very same, the incarnation itself—the fact that God chose to have a mother—that proves true the audacious claim: God does indeed value women." *Women and the Gender of God* (Grand Rapids, MI: Eerdmans, 2022), 7. For a full treatment of this question, see Peeler's fifth chapter.

[4]Charles Marsh, *Evangelical Anxiety: A Memoir* (San Francisco: HarperOne, 2022), 153.

[5]I don't mean there are no asexual people. In contemporary culture, we may use the term *asexual* to refer to someone with no pronounced experience of sexual desire or no felt association with a particular gender norm, category of sexual orientation, or identity. People like this absolutely exist, and their accounts of their own experiences should be taken seriously. I also do not mean that every person's body maps perfectly onto the pervasive sex binary between male and female. The concept of someone's body being "intersex," existing somewhere on a spectrum between male and female is also a reality Christians and pastors should take seriously. However, I would argue that even intersex bodies are not *asexual* but rather, as the term implies, *intersexual*. See Bridget Eileen Rivera, *Heavy Burdens: Seven Ways LGBTQ Christians Experience Harm in the Church* (Grand Rapids, MI: Brazos, 2021), 144-58, for a helpful and potentially challenging discussion of intersexuality and gender identity. Some have speculated that Jesus himself was asexual in the sense that he didn't experience erotic desire in the way many people do. We have no way of knowing one way or the other, but even this does not mean that his body was asexual. We have every reason to affirm that Jesus' body was male, penis and all.

[6]With sincere apologies to Dan Brown and Martin Scorsese, there is no meaningful historical evidence Jesus had a sexual relationship with Mary Magdalene.

[7]The nature of sin's relationship to desire and goodness has been a point of discussion and debate throughout church history. A helpful tradition understands sin as a "privation" or twisting of the good. In this model, all our human capacities, including our bodily desires, were created good and would have been directed only toward good ends before Adam and Eve's fall. Sin bends our innate goodness toward evil, corrupting our wills and even our ways of desiring. A theology of the corruption of sexual desire is often associated with Saint Augustine and his teaching on concupiscence. For a technical discussion, see Timo Nisula, *Augustine and the Functions of Concupiscence* (Leiden, Netherlands: Brill, 2012), 69-135. On an Augustinian view, Jesus' humanity was not

subject to the will-corrupting influence of original sin and thus, presumably, would have experienced sexual desire in a different way than fallen humans. A counter point to this view may follow the reasoning of Gregory Nazianzen's famous statement, "What has not been assumed has not been healed." Some argue this means Jesus experienced the full weight of fallen human nature. I am more sympathetic to this view. What we can say with confidence is that whatever Jesus' experience of sexual desire was like, it was holy and sinless. In summary, I would argue that sexual desire in and of itself is not evil but has been bent and twisted by sin. For a secular account of how the critique of desire relates to sexual ethics, see Christine Emba's chapter "Some Desires Are Worse Than Others" in Christine Emba, *Rethinking Sex: A Provocation* (New York: Sentinel, 2022), 133-57.

[8]This is not to suggest that the premodern church is not without its own excesses and imbalances on sex and gender. It's not a stretch to say the ancient church was worse than contemporary evangelical emphases on sexual purity. But that's not the topic of this book!

8. BEFORE YOU KNEW YOU WERE SEXUAL

[1]Nate Pyle, *Man Enough: How Jesus Redefines Manhood* (Grand Rapids, MI: Zondervan, 2015), 153.

[2]Not every heroic male character is like this. A happy exception is Frodo in *The Lord of the Rings*.

[3]People have different definitions of what counts as porn, and recall bias makes it difficult to trust surveys asking people to volunteer the exact age when they first saw a pornographic image or video. Structuring randomized, statistically reliable studies to answer this question is challenging for these and other reasons. It is fair to say that prepubescent exposure is common, but knowing the exact age when this happens, on average, is not as straightforward. I'm indebted to an online exchange with sociologist Samuel Perry for these insights. You can read some of his research on pornography in *Addicted to Lust: Pornography in the Lives of Conservative Protestants* (New York: Oxford University Press, 2019).

[4]Andrew Peterson, *The God of the Garden: Thoughts on Creation, Culture, and the Kingdom* (Nashville: B&H, 2021), 10.

9. FROM FIGHT TO FORMATION

[1]This distress continues to be felt by many adult Christian men. See Samuel Perry, *Addicted to Lust: Pornography in the Lives of Conservative Protestants* (New York: Oxford University Press, 2019), 72. On page 75, he writes, "The experience of morally rejecting pornography but viewing it anyway (however infrequently) led to depression for American men."

[2]Jay Stringer, *Unwanted: How Sexual Brokenness Reveals Our Way to Healing* (Colorado Springs: NavPress, 2018), 100.

[3]In a 2021 interview, pop superstar Billie Eilish said, "As a woman, I think porn is a disgrace. I used to watch a lot of porn, to be honest. I started watching porn when I was like 11." She went on, "I think it really destroyed my brain and I feel incredibly devastated that I was exposed to so much porn." Elisha Fieldstadt, "Billie Eilish Reveals She Watched Porn at Young Age, Calls It 'A Disgrace,'" *NBC News*, December 15, 2021, www.nbcnews.com/news/us-news/billie-eilish -reveals-watched-porn-young-age-calls-disgrace-rcna8863. Eilish's comments made international headlines, not least because she transgressed a pro-porn stance assumed by many social progressives. *Teen Vogue*, for instance, in an article covering Eilish's interview, tried to qualify her comments. See Brittney McNamara, "Billie Eilish Opened Up About Porn and Mental Health," *Teen Vogue*, December 15, 2021, www.teenvogue.com/story/billie-eilish-porn-and -mental-health.

[4]Johnny Walsh, "Nadia Bolz-Weber Does Ministry Differently," *Out in Jersey*, October 21, 2018, https://outinjersey.net/nadia-bolz-weber-does-ministry -differently. See also Nadia Bolz-Weber, *Shameless: A Sexual Reformation* (New York: Convergent, 2019), 135-48.

[5]Bolz-Weber, *Shameless,* 145.

[6]See Stringer, *Unwanted,* 127-37.

[7]As Carl Trueman writes, "There is no way to tell the difference between pornography involving willing participants and that which is essentially a recording of a rape" in *The Rise and Triumph of the Modern Self: Cultural Amnesia, Expressive Individualism, and the Road to Sexual Revolution* (Wheaton, IL: Crossway, 2020), 286. As a possible counter to Trueman's claim, sites like OnlyFans seek to reverse the power imbalances in pornography and give the "actors" ownership and control over the content they produce, creating a structure where it is more coherent to claim someone has consented to their likeness being used in pornography. However, I do not subscribe to a consent-only sexual ethic, and the other concerns about disembodied and non-relational sexuality remain. Likewise, this does nothing to address systemic issues of an unjust pornographic culture that preys on minors both as actors and consumers. Nor does it account for the ways that pornography shapes young people toward self-gratifying and dehumanizing sexual behavior later in life.

[8]Stringer, *Unwanted,* 39.

[9]As a side note, the Greek word often translated "lust" in the New Testament (*epithymia/epithymeō*) does not have an overt sexual connotation. Sometimes it

is used this way, but often it refers to a non-sinful desire or generic (not necessarily sexual) sinful desire.

[10] On this point see Jonathan Grant's discussion of a letter sent by C. S. Lewis to Keith Masson, from the Wade Center archive at Wheaton College, quoted in Jonathan Grant, *Divine Sex: A Compelling Vision for Christian Relationships in a Hypersexualized Age* (Grand Rapids, MI: Brazos, 2015), 111.

[11] See Bridget Eileen Rivera, *Heavy Burdens: Seven Ways LGBTQ Christians Experience Harm in the Church* (Grand Rapids: Brazos, 2021).

10. YOU SAY GOODBYE, I SAY HELLO

[1] This is not her real name.

[2] This is also not her real name.

[3] What's sometimes not appreciated about the Elliots' story is how Jim *mistreated* Elisabeth and used his commitment to the Lord to excuse stringing her along. Sheila Wray Gregoire, "On Elisabeth Elliot's Terrible Courtship—and Dating Men 'Sold Out for Jesus,'" *Bare Marriage* (blog), July 26, 2021, https://baremarriage.com/2021/07/on-elisabeth-elliots-terrible-courtship-and-dating-men-sold-out-for-jesus/.

[4] Debra Hirsch, *Redeeming Sex: Naked Conversations About Sexuality and Spirituality* (Downers Grove, IL: InterVarsity Press, 2015), 37.

[5] For further resources on the fixation on virginity, see Christine Gardner, *Making Chastity Sexy: The Rhetoric of Evangelical Abstinence Campaigns* (Berkeley: University of California Press, 2011); Jessica Valenti, *The Purity Myth: How America's Obsession with Virginity Is Hurting Young Women* (Cypress, CA: Seal Press, 2009); and Rachel Joy Welcher, *Talking Back to Purity Culture: Rediscovering Faithful Christian Sexuality* (Downers Grove, IL: InterVarsity Press, 2019), 19-30.

[6] Curt Thompson, *The Soul of Desire: Discovering the Neuroscience of Longing, Beauty, and Community* (Downers Grove, IL: InterVarsity Press, 2021), 21.

[7] Thomas Merton, *Love and Living*, ed. Naomi Burton Stone and Patrick Hart (New York: Farrar, Straus, and Giroux, 1979), 27.

11. ACT LIKE AN ADULT

[1] The experience was especially painful for her because she is a survivor of childhood sexual abuse. Though she didn't understand the extent of the abuse at the time, it retraumatized her being told men in the church were sexualizing her.

[2] I'm not even making a point here about whether male-only eldership is biblical. Every problem I've noted in this paragraph could be addressed and mitigated within a complementarian church. One church I'm familiar with created a women's council to serve as the mothers for the congregation. The council was

created to hold the elders accountable to the needs of women in the congregation and to give the elders much-needed female input in their decision-making and leadership.

[3]I'm indebted in this paragraph to a conversation with my friend Joe Jackowski.

[4]As a side note, the low-church contexts where accountability groups are most common often don't allow space for a congregational confession of sin during worship. Liturgical confession is public but also vague and anonymous. It brings sinners into contact with the assurances of God's forgiveness and encourages them toward holy living. However, it does this without the embarrassment and shame that can often accompany confession in accountability groups. Additionally, absolution and assurance of forgiveness are often not a feature of accountability groups at all.

[5]Denny Burk, "What's in a Name? The Meaning and Origin of 'Complementarian,'" The Council for Biblical Manhood and Womanhood, August 1, 2019, https://cbmw.org/2019/08/01/whats-in-a-name.

[6]For a recent historical overview of this debate, see Beth Allison Barr, The Making of Biblical Womanhood: How the Subjugation of Women Became Gospel Truth (Grand Rapids, MI: Brazos, 2021). The complementarian position is most famously outlined in Recovering Biblical Manhood and Womanhood: A Response to Evangelical Feminism, ed. John Piper and Wayne Grudem (Wheaton, IL: Crossway, 1991).

[7]Kate Shellnut, "Willow Creek Investigation: Allegations Against Bill Hybels Are Credible," Christianity Today, February 28, 2019, www.christianitytoday.com/news/2019/february/willow-creek-bill-hybels-investigation-iag-report.html.

[8]In all of this, we were influenced by the work of Wesley Hill in Spiritual Friendship: Finding Love in the Church as a Celibate Gay Christian (Grand Rapids, MI: Brazos, 2015). While none of us identified as LGBTQ+, we were greatly helped by the premise that the church should be a place where both married and single Christians can create friendships with family-like intimacy.

12. THE WORST SEX YOU'VE EVER HAD

[1]Charles Marsh, Evangelical Anxiety: A Memoir (San Francisco: HarperOne, 2022), 96.

[2]For example, Marsh, Evangelical Anxiety, 95-97; and Linda Kay Klein, Pure: Inside the Evangelical Movement That Shamed a Generation of Women and How I Broke Free (New York: Atria, 2022), 135-37, 186-89.

[3]See Rachel Joy Welcher's chapter "Virginity as Identity" in Talking Back to Purity Culture: Rediscovering Faithful Christian Sexuality (Downers Grove, IL: InterVarsity Press, 2019), 19-30.

13. LEARNING TO LOVE

[1] The term *incel* is short for "involuntary celibate," referring to a reclusive online community of men embittered against the women of society who won't have sex with them.

[2] For more on unhelpful readings of 1 Corinthians 7, see Sheila Wray Gregoire, Rebecca Gregoire Lindenbach, and Joanna Sawatsky's *The Great Sex Rescue: The Lies You've Been Taught and How to Recover What God Intended* (Grand Rapids, MI: Baker, 2021), 153-55.

[3] Driscoll has since softened his rhetoric on this point, avoiding gendered language and instead using more neutral terms like "high-sex-drive spouse" or "low-sex-drive spouse." But the message of accommodating your sexual frequency to a partner's appetite for porn and/or masturbation remains the same. See Mark and Grace Driscoll, "How Often Should We Have Sex?" April 12, 2021, in *Real Marriage*, podcast, XO Marriage, https://xomarriage.com/podcasts/real-marriage/.

[4] Thomas Merton, *Love and Living*, ed. Naomi Burton Stone and Patrick Hart (New York: Farrar, Straus, and Giroux, 1979), 34.

[5] Christine Emba, *Rethinking Sex: A Provocation* (New York: Sentinel, 2022), 165.

[6] Jay Stringer, *Unwanted: How Sexual Brokenness Reveals Our Way to Healing* (Colorado Springs: NavPress, 2018), 113.

[7] bell hooks, *All About Love: New Visions* (New York: William Morrow, 2001), 159.

[8] If you're looking for how-to books on improving your sexual intimacy from a Christian perspective, there are none I would recommend more than Sheila Gregoire's *The Great Sex Rescue* and *The Good Guy's Guide to Great Sex: Because Good Guys Make the Best Lovers* (Grand Rapids, MI: Zondervan, 2022).

14. FATHERHOOD

[1] This theological tradition is summarized well by Jonathan Grant, *Divine Sex: A Compelling Vision for Christian Relationships in a Hypersexualized Age* (Grand Rapids, MI: Brazos, 2015), 152-56.

[2] For an accessible introduction and overview of recent Catholic teaching on sexuality, see Christopher West, *Our Bodies Tell God's Story: Discovering the Divine Plan for Love, Sex, and Gender* (Grand Rapids, MI: Brazos, 2020), which is itself a distillation of Pope John Paul II, *Man and Woman He Created Them: A Theology of the Body* (Boston: Pauline Books, 2006). See also J. Budziszewski, *On the Meaning of Sex* (Wilmington, DE: Intercollegiate Studies Institute, 2014).

[3] This is a general point about the way bodies work. There are scientific workarounds like sperm donors, IVF, or surrogacy. I also acknowledge that some people who identify as men may not have the reproductive capacities of

cisgendered men. Despite this, I would argue that even these nontraditional modes of fathering a child still base their pattern and possibility for new human life on the normative union of a sperm and an ovum from a male and a female body.

[4]Curt Thompson, *The Soul of Desire: Discovering the Neuroscience of Longing, Beauty, and Community* (Downers Grove, IL: InterVarsity Press, 2021), 33.

[5]Grant, *Divine Sex*, 71.

15. DEATH AND RESURRECTION

[1]The many cultural revolutions of dignity and liberation brought about through Christianity are the subject of Tom Holland's excellent book, *Dominion: The Making of the Western Mind* (London: Little, Brown, 2019).

[2]C. S. Lewis, *The Great Divorce*, C. S. Lewis Signature Classics Edition (London: William Collins, 2012), ix.

[3]See Suzannah Weiss, "These Christian Leaders Embraced Sex Positivity—and Now Preach It," *Washington Post*, April 20, 2022, www.washingtonpost.com /lifestyle/2022/04/20/christian-leaders-sex-positivity.

[4]Curt Thompson, *The Soul of Desire: Discovering the Neuroscience of Longing, Beauty, and Community* (Downers Grove, IL: InterVarsity Press, 2021), 24.

[5]"The Principles of the Third Order," The Third Order, Society of St. Francis, accessed September 6, 2022, https://tssf.org.uk/about-the-third-order/the -principles-of-the-third-order.